Library Service Design

LIBRARY INFORMATION TECHNOLOGY ASSOCIATION (LITA) GUIDES

Marta Mestrovic Deyrup, Ph.D.
Acquisitions Editor, Library Information and Technology Association,
a division of the American Library Association

The Library Information Technology Association (LITA) Guides provide information and guidance on topics related to cutting edge technology for library and IT specialists.

Written by top professionals in the field of technology, the guides are sought after by librarians wishing to learn a new skill or to become current in today's best practices.

Each book in the series has been overseen editorially since conception by LITA and reviewed by LITA members with special expertise in the specialty area of the book.

Established in 1966, the Library and Information Technology Association (LITA) is the division of the American Library Association (ALA) that provides its members and the library and information science community as a whole with a forum for discussion, an environment for learning, and a program for actions on the design, development, and implementation of automated and technological systems in the library and information science field.

Approximately 25 LITA Guides were published by Neal-Schuman and ALA between 2007 and 2015. Rowman & Littlefield took over publication of the series beginning in late 2015. Books in the series published by Rowman & Littlefield are:

1. *Digitizing Flat Media: Principles and Practices*
2. *The Librarian's Introduction to Programming Languages*
3. *Library Service Design: A LITA Guide to Holistic Assessment, Insight, and Improvement*

Library Service Design

A LITA Guide to Holistic Assessment, Insight, and Improvement

Joe J. Marquez and Annie Downey

ROWMAN & LITTLEFIELD
Lanham • Boulder • New York • London

Published by Rowman & Littlefield
A wholly owned subsidiary of The Rowman & Littlefield Publishing Group, Inc.
4501 Forbes Boulevard, Suite 200, Lanham, Maryland 20706
www.rowman.com

Unit A, Whitacre Mews, 26-34 Stannary Street, London SE11 4AB

British Library Cataloguing in Publication Information Available

Library of Congress Cataloging-in-Publication Data Available

ISBN 978-1-4422-6383-3 (hardcover : alk. paper)
ISBN 978-1-4422-6384-0 (pbk : alk. paper)
ISBN 978-1-4422-6385-7 (ebook)

♾™ The paper used in this publication meets the minimum requirements of American
National Standard for Information Sciences Permanence of Paper for Printed Library
Materials, ANSI/NISO Z39.48-1992.

Printed in the United States of America

For Korey, Beni, and Theo

For Maggie Anne, Livvie, and Sophie

Contents

Illustrations

Preface

PURPOSE

Library Service Design: A LITA Guide to Holistic Assessment, Insight, and Improvement covers all things service design in libraries. The purpose is to introduce and educate readers about the service design methodology and tools. The genesis of this book was our Library User Experience (LUX) team being asked to look at redesigning our library website. This quickly grew to include looking at our physical touchpoints and eventually to understanding how space was being used throughout the library. At that point, we needed a design methodology that could "see" beyond a single touchpoint. We discovered service design through the process of looking for a method to evaluate the library holistically. After seeing how well it worked in our environment and how useful service design was for assessing and refining library services, we decided it was too good not to share.

Until now, libraries have not had a reliable and holistic method for assessing services and resources. Attend any conference and you will see a hodge-podge of methods and how they have worked for specific environments. In recent years, we have seen the introduction of usability studies, anthropological methods, and a focus on qualitative methods for better understanding our users. Words like *ethnography* and *user experience* have entered the librarian's lexicon. There are now entire tracks at conferences dedicated to the usability of library websites and catalog interfaces. But the user's experience is more than just a single interaction with an interface. If you believe this, as we do, *Library Service Design* is for you.

This is not a cookbook of recipes. It does not prescribe how to conduct a service design research project. The good thing is that there is no one way. The bad thing is that there is no one way. We have organized the content into sections that can be read from cover to cover, or as needed. Piece things together. Mix and match. Combine tools and processes with other methodologies. Do your best and what works for your library and team.

AUDIENCE

This book was written by librarians for librarians and library staff to rethink how we currently view library services. At the time of this writing, service design and methods related to design thinking are not unfamiliar in the private sector, but are only now getting much needed press time among librarians and in library literature and media. Librarianship, at its heart, is about service delivery. What better way to rethink our services than through an evidence-based design methodology.

HOW THE BOOK IS ORGANIZED

This book is comprised of three distinct sections. The first section (chapters 1 and 2) is a primer for understanding service design. We look at what service design is, as well as what a service entails. It sets the stage for understanding why we need "another" methodology. The second section (chapters 3 and 4) explains what service design looks like in action. This section is about the phases of service design, as well as the tools. And the last section (chapters 5 and 6) is about owning service design, adapting it to your library, and what you can look forward to when using a service design methodology.

BOOK DETAILS

At its core, service design is about thinking in systems and seeing how tightly coupled the various library components are. In chapter 1, we explain how making a change to one component affects other components. It is hard to think of a library component that might exist on its own. Yet, when assessing service delivery, we often examine various parts in isolation from other services. It is time to change this habit. In the first chapter, we also discuss how users experience the library. Working to understand how users think and feel is the first step in discovering how to deliver better services that evolve as they do.

Library Service Design is not just about service design as a methodology, but also service design as a mindset. In chapter 2, we also look at the service design mindset, which will help librarians think differently about how they deliver and offer services. With service design, services are everything and everywhere in the library. As such, they need to be managed, assessed, measured, and, at times, redesigned to accommodate the library's current users. Evaluating and rethinking services is not just done *for* users, but *with* them. This is what separates service design from other design methodologies.

Service design is a methodology conducted in multiple phases. In chapter 3, we give details on what those phases look like and what tools work best for each. The phases are categorized according to the various goals for each one. Not every project will use the same tools, but we highlight our favorites in chapter 4. Mix and match using the tools that will help answer your research question and work for your library and your team. At the end of the day, you really do know what will work best for your project in your library.

Throughout the book, we provide examples from our own experience using service design at Reed College Library. These examples are simply what worked for us. Your library is different, and we encourage you to adapt the information provided here to fit your library's culture and context (see chapter 5). An important part of adapting service design for your facility is creating a research team that reflects the departments and people in your library. We review how to create internal and external teams. We also discuss the importance of owning the process and being transparent so your colleagues understand what you are doing, as well as what you are not doing.

Chapter 6 is about looking forward. Too often, we discover a great new thing at a conference and return to our home library ready to implement what we have learned, only to find that the project ends and life returns to "normal." The final chapter offers ideas for making service design assessment part of your library's culture and ongoing assessment "something we do," like changing the toner in the printers or checking out books at the circulation desk. Finally, we argue that service design should be more commonly used as an assessment methodology in libraries.

HOW TO USE THIS BOOK

Library Service Design is a manual for implementing a service design methodology in your library. It is designed to help you understand this complex, multifaceted, yet easy, way to implement methodology. It will alter the way you see your library and your users giving you greater insight into the assessment of the entire library. It offers both a mindset and a set of tools to guide you through your own library service design project. You may read the tools section and only want to use the Customer Journey Map. Using one tool is great if it helps you become more familiar with your library system, users, and services. What you might find is that not only is the Customer Journey Map a powerful tool for seeing the library as a whole, but it inspired you to want to explore one or more aspects of the customer journey in depth. You can combine tools to help see the bigger picture, but they can also be used individually. One of the powers of service design is its ability to scale. You can focus on a smaller section of your facility, but the results will still show the impact of the entire library on that smaller section. This is by design and is important in understanding how resources are used and how any change impacts the entire library system.

As you read the book, we ask that you approach the methodology with an open mind. The ideas may challenge the way you think about the various processes in your library. We dare you to ask, "Why do we do things that way?" If the answer is, "We've always done it that way," then this book is for you. A certain service or process may not have been updated since the cornerstone for your library was laid. It might be time to adapt your library to today's user, not the users that were the first to use its services. Service design opens up a new way to look at the library for what it is, not what we think it should be.

LAST WORD

We didn't invent service design. Our goal was to take this accepted methodology and introduce it to libraries. At the present time, the library literature contains only a handful of articles on service design (one of which we wrote). So, we decided to write the book on it. If you want to read more about service design, please use the references at the back of the book. They not only support the various points in the book, but also provide a reading list for librarians interested in pursuing service design in their libraries. Considering that we are a service industry, it makes sense for libraries and librarians to be familiar with a methodology that looks at services from the user's perspective. We hope you agree.

Acknowledgments

This book is the product of much thinking, reading, and breathing of services. We wish to acknowledge those who helped shape our thoughts about the concepts presented here. For those we've left off the list . . . please blame Joe.

First, we would like to thank the members of Reed's Library User Experience (LUX) group, Linda Maddux, Eric Alwine, and Ryan Clement. The work of LUX is truly a team effort and is both fun and interesting. There may be no better team of "adults" to have multiple slices of pizza (or sushi) with while talking to students. The work of LUX was made possible through the efforts of the LUX Student Working Group. We would especially like to thank Emma, Vikram, and Pema for sticking with us for so long. Your thoughtfulness, efforts, and devotion to the work has been inspiring. Here's to a fireplace in the Ref Room (one day). The efforts of LUX were, in part, the idea of Dena Hutto, Reed College librarian. Her contributions from day 1 have been greatly appreciated. We can always count on Dena to provide thoughtful guidance and feedback. Her dedication to providing the best possible library experience for students is what allows us to do our work.

We have made many friends as a result of our evangelizing about service design. Our first editors at *Weave: Journal of Library User Experience*, Matthew Reidsma and Kyle Felker, gave service design in libraries a platform. Kris Johnson of Montana State University was a willing comrade in spreading the word about service design in libraries. Thanks for your support and for getting the word out. Kirstin Hierholzer and Lesli Larson of the University of Oregon Libraries gave us the opportunity to turn our little project into a "thing." Christine Tawatao, Courtney McDonald, and Rebecca Blakiston were supportive of our efforts throughout our endeavors. Many thanks to Rory Litwin of Library Juice for providing space in the curriculum to help spread the word.

Charles Harmon was always patient (even with Joe's many e-mails) and encouraging about the content on these pages. He shepherded our project to where it is today. Thanks to the staff at Rowman & Littlefield for their help with our book. We would also like to recognize the folks at LITA who were able to see the benefits of service design in a library setting, Marta M. Deyrup and Tom Wilson. And many thanks to Patrick Hogan at ALA, who also saw the advantages of service design and hopes to build on what we started.

And last, thank you to our colleagues and students at Reed College Library for making our library environment a supportive and fun place to work. With all the parts working together, we can make for a unified system. Thanks for allowing us to be a part of it.

Joe would like to thank Professor Ellen West of Portland State University School of Business for introducing him to Design Thinking, which led to the "discovery" of service design. Your undying support and kind words have been invaluable. Rick Robison, thank you for the great conversations when we can find the time (I think you owe me a couple of beers, though). Thanks to my sisters, Monica and Rosalie, for supporting their little brother. I am grateful for Charlie, Jack, Addie, and Sam, for being "model" nephews and niece. To my parents, Joe and Carmen, thank you for always cheering from the sideline. Cindee Egge, I appreciate your constant help and presence. Thank you Beni and Theo for being yourselves (and for being the best sons a Dibs could have). And, last, I'd like to give a huge thank you to my wife Korey for always keeping our family grounded. We can't say thank you enough for all you do.

Annie would like to thank Gayla Byerly and Dena Hutto, the best mentors a person could hope for. In addition to the many, many things Gayla has done for me, she also introduced me to the importance and power of assessment. There are not enough words of thanks for Gayla. Since my very first meeting with Dena, I have been impressed by her professionalism, intellect, and compassion. She is a true visionary. Thanks to my sister Kendra and my brothers Andrew and Jesse. I feel immensely lucky to be a Keefer sibling. My mother, Margie Jones-Keefer, has always believed in and encouraged me. I try to be as good as she seems to think I am and make her proud. My beautiful daughters, Maggie Anne, Livvie, and Sophie, are a source of constant inspiration. Thank you for being so uniquely you. And finally, Mike, you are my second brain, my biggest fan, and my true soul mate. Thank you for all that you do every day.

Chapter One

The Case for Service Design in Libraries, or Libraries as Systems

More than fifty years ago, famed industrial designer Henry Dreyfuss wrote the following:

> It must constantly be borne in mind that the object being worked on is going to be ridden in, sat upon, looked at, talked into, activated, operated, or in some way used by people individually or en masse. *If the point of contact between the product and people becomes a point of friction, then the designer has failed.* If, on the other hand, people are made safer, more comfortable, more desirous of purchase, more efficient—or just plain happier—by contact with the product, then the designer has succeeded. [1]

Dreyfuss knew his business. As a designer, he focused on the human element and the necessity of designing for people. His work ranged from designing phones, thermostats, and alarm clocks to tractors, trains, and even stationary. He created an international sourcebook of more than twenty thousand symbols that are the standard symbols used by industrial designers throughout the world even today. Dreyfuss's innovative, yet simple and user-friendly, designs still impact how we work and live. The lessons he taught designers are just as relevant now as they were fifty years ago, and they are equally relevant to the work libraries are doing to try to make and keep their services useful, relevant, and meaningful for users. As a user-centered service profession, librarianship has a lot to learn from Dreyfuss. Our role as service providers should be to eliminate those "points of friction" that appear between our users and our library systems, services, and people. While this is not a book about Henry Dreyfuss or his work per se, the lessons he taught serve as inspiration for our work in researching, designing, and maintaining core and innovative services in libraries.

Service design is unique in that it looks at everything we do and provide in the library as a service. It not only looks at how space and resources are allocated and integrated into the library ecology, but also how they are consumed by the user. Because libraries and the objects contained therein are constantly "ridden in, sat upon, looked at, talked into, activated, operated . . . [and] used by people," it is incumbent on librarians to ensure that we locate and eliminate points of friction and find ways to delight our users. Creating user-centered services in libraries is not new; however, in the last decade, we have seen a fundamental shift in user demand, "from the expectation of functional performance to a more broadly satisfying experience."[2] As our economy moves away from being based on manufacturing to services (and experiences), there is an increasing need to ensure that users are satisfied with the products and services they interact with. Service design can help us do that by providing tools and a pathway for understanding what users want, expect, and need from a specific library so we can properly assess our services.[3]

Service design is unique in that it is a holistic, user-centered, systems-based approach that involves actual users throughout the entire process of designing, implementing, and assessing services. It is an especially powerful and useful methodology for librarians because it is grounded in systems thinking, which demands that we look at the entire library ecology when designing services. It also requires that we take the typical objects and products we provide to users and look at them as services, which suddenly gives tables, lamps, outlets, collections, computers, and other objects more meaning. This view of how resources are used provides insight into how our users experience the library. Finally, service design helps library workers break down the silos that not only hurt the quality of service users experience, but also can damage morale and limit the ability of managers to develop a happy, cohesive, and satisfied staff.

This book is an overview of and manual on how to begin using service design in your library. In this chapter, we make the case for service design as a powerful and meaningful method for creating, refining, and assessing library services.

THE LIBRARY IS A SYSTEM

Libraries are composed of interconnected elements (see figure 1.1) that work to fulfill the purpose of helping users meet their information needs. Like all systems, libraries consist of a "set of elements that [are] coherently organized in a way that achieves something."[4] But those of us working in libraries do not usually think of the entire library system when we do our work because to create manageable departments, libraries have been broken down by task and function, which often results in the feeling that we work in silos and a loss of our "intrinsic sense of connection to a larger whole."[5]

Users are also not aware that the library is a system because they experience it as a physical building that houses books, tables, and staff that they know as librarians or an online hub with databases, ebooks, and other electronic resources. They see and experience the library as a whole. They often don't realize that the library is divided into smaller departments formed around staff job duties. The departments, which are named similarly to the

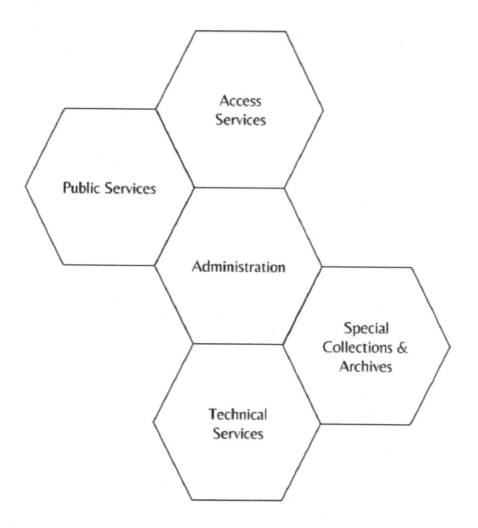

Figure 1.1.   The library as a tightly coupled system.

tasks or duties they perform, appear on the organization chart in small boxes. These boxes often become the silos of the library. The employees in a silo focus only on their tasks and don't look at the other silos unless a user's need forces them to refer a patron elsewhere. This is typical of how most organizations work. Each person is assigned tasks, they do them, and that's it. Unfortunately (or fortunately), library users are removed enough from library employees' work tasks that they don't usually see them. But the bad news is they often experience the result of this siloing, even if they don't realize it is impacting them.

To avoid users being negatively affected by our division of labor, we need to begin thinking of the library as a system, with its associated elements and interconnections. From this perspective, it is clear that the function or purpose of the various pieces working together creates the overall user experience. For example, just within the simple task of finding and checking out a book, a user experiences the wholeness of the library—the elements that work together to create a single experience: They use the catalog that catalogers have created and maintain, which has been embedded on a website created by public services staff; they speak to a reference librarian about how to find the book; they wander the stacks and pull the book from neatly organized shelves; and they check the book out from a staff member working at the circulation desk. While completing this process, the user experiences the library as a whole, taking advantage of the work of many to find and check out a book. They do not see the invisible lines that divide the library by task and function.

Viewing the library as a system provides us with a total view of the experience and reminds us of the original purpose and nature of the library, rather than what it has become for management purposes. Services do not function inside a vacuum,[6] but are tightly coupled with other services created by the library. Looking at the library from a systems perspective puts the emphasis back on the user's total experience rather than focusing on the siloed completion of tasks. For staff members, the compartmentalized tasks may still be in the forefront of things to be done behind the scenes, but from the user's perspective, completing each task plays just one part in creating their overall experience.

How Did We Get Here?

In 1911, Frederick Taylor published his highly influential text *The Principles of Scientific Management*, in which he called for a change in how we manage workers and work.[7] He emphasized something he referred to as "task management," or scientific management, with the goal of creating levels of efficiency in daily operations. Taylor's idea took off and has permeated the American organizational landscape. People bought into this idea, and we have been chasing the clock (and our tails) in the name of efficiency ever since. Task management not only spread through the manufacturing world, but it also dictated the structure of most organizations, including libraries. While the underlying systems have been in place throughout, Taylorism obscured the whole and replaced it with compartmentalized silos based on tasks.

In addition to understanding tasks in light of systems, it is also helpful to consider that systems are "interconnected in such a way that they produce their own pattern of behavior over time."[8] Libraries are systems with unique functions and behavior; to understand them, we need to study and observe how they behave and function.[9] Like most nonprofit and educational organizations, libraries are driven by mission statements. But "purposes are deduced from behavior, not from rhetoric or stated goals."[10] In this way, users do not care what our mission statements say—they learn our true purpose by how the library staff behaves and how well the system functions.

Adjusting Interconnections

We can see the coupled nature of library tasks by adjusting the interconnections. Imagine the following scenario: You work at a large university library that has been experiencing the mid-fall sickness that descends on the library staff and student workers each year. Books are being turned in faster than your staff can get them back on the shelves. An industrious student worker does not know you are shorthanded in shelving so he quickly checks the books in as they arrive. He takes off for class while the books sit on a truck near the circulation desk for the entire day.

Meanwhile, a student named Anna meets with her professor about a paper that is due the following morning. Anna's professor recommends that she use a specific book to fill out some ideas in her writing. Prior to heading to the library in the rain, Anna checks the library catalog from her dorm room to see if the book is available. Since it has been checked in, the catalog states that it is on the shelf. Anna walks across campus to the library. She looks for the book on the shelf. It is not there so she goes to the reference desk to ask for help. The librarian walks with her to the stacks and the reshelving area to look for the book. They cannot find it, so they go to the circulation desk and fill out a missing book card so someone will look for the book. The student worker at circulation takes the card, and Anna leaves the library feeling dissatisfied with her experience. All the while, the book she needs was sitting on a book truck next to the circulation desk.

It is easy to see how one wrong move can impact the overall system and the user experience. Anna was understandably frustrated by the missing resource, and her frustration was likely exacerbated by being taken to various service points and not getting what she really needed. Anna has used the library many times, and although the overall purpose of the library remains the same, her experience was altered by the fact that there were delays in the system where there previously had been none, at least not without some level of communication as to why something was happening.

Decisions in Isolation

Another reason to view the library as a system is to lessen the impact of decisions made in isolation. Meyer and Schwager write, "[C]ustomer experience encompasses every aspect of a [library's] offering . . . yet few of the people responsible for those things have given sustained thought to how their separate decisions shape customer experience."[11] Without thinking of the library and its elements as integrated for a purpose larger than departmental tasks, decisions can be made that impact service and the overall user experience. An easy example is when a change to the library website is made without consulting other departments. We know that staff working at service desks use the website extensively when they work with patrons. Making changes without consulting them can damage the impression users have of the service desk staff and the overall user experience. This is true for less visible parts of the system as well. Thinking and deciding in isolation impacts the greater purpose. This is not to say that every decision needs to be a consensus, but it requires that the actors communicate and think beyond their silos.

Looking at the library as a system allows you to not only notice the interconnections and the reliance of each department on other departments, but also leads to a better understanding of the overall purpose of the library and opens the way to designing the experiences according to the purpose and user expectations. We can make ordinary tasks into a seamless experience by working together.[12] A user's experience doesn't end when one department performs their task well.[13] It is only when we look at the library through the eyes of the user that we can truly see past the silos and departmental barriers we've created and understand the seamless behavior users demand and expect.

This book is a call to librarians and library workers to take back our library systems. When we take a step back and see the parts working together, the system and the experience of both producers and consumers takes shape. Through the lens of the user experience, it is clear that this "optimizing for efficiency through specialization eventually compromises overall effectiveness."[14] The emphasis on being efficient can remove the library staff from the reason we are here in the first place. Consequently, optimizing the user and staff experience—while not getting overly bogged down by each miniscule task—will lead to a happier and better-functioning library system.

THE LIBRARY FROM THE USER'S PERSPECTIVE, OR IS EVERYONE HERE A LIBRARIAN?

When a user walks into the library, they do not see the embodied version of an organization chart. Instead, they experience a temperature-controlled, well-lighted facility with desks, tables, chairs, stacks, and friendly people to assist them in finding appropriate resources and help them check things out. If they are walking into a newer facility, they may experience varying levels of noise, as determined by a learning commons layout, or if they are entering an older library, they may be enveloped by a rich sense of history and quiet. And in their eyes, everyone is a librarian. They see the library as a holistic experience, complete with stimuli that engage the senses through smell, sound, sight, touch, and thermoception. They don't see the imposed barriers from the organizational and management structure.

Imagine a user needing to print something, but the printer jams or is offline. In seeking help, the first person they encounter may be a librarian at the reference desk or a paraprofessional at circulation. When they ask for help and the librarian or paraprofessional responds that they don't know how to fix the printer because printing is handled by the IT department, the user leaves frustrated. This user doesn't see organization charts or job descriptions; they only see people working in a library who cannot or will not help. For the user, "distinction lies less in the processes which operate and more in the way those processes are shaped into a coherent form."[15] Users only see what is in front of them. Thus, to understand users, librarians need to study and understand the "coherent form" of the library experience and how users understand that form.

UNDERSTANDING THE USER AND USER EXPECTATIONS

People come to libraries with "jobs to be done"[16] and expectations of how well the library will meet their needs. Some of these expectations are based on prior experiences with similar functionality.[17] Perhaps they've gone shopping online and ordered a book or two, or they've made reservations at a restaurant and it worked out well. These external experiences with technology and services influence their library expectations. They think that if task X worked well in one environment, it should work in another environment. Users have a tendency to cluster similar experiences together.[18] As a result, expectations can be based on what the user perceives as a similar service.

Another important aspect to consider is the emotional attachment users place on a space. In time, they develop a level of familiarity with how a service is performed and assign a level of emotional attachment, which influences how and when they access a service. Attachment to a place develops slowly, and is never in passing.[19] Attachment comes in two forms, *place dependence* and *place identity*. Place dependence refers to the "importance of a place in providing features and conditions that support specific goals."[20] Place identity is the "symbolic importance of a place as a repository for emotions."[21] In both instances, the user assigns personal meaning to a space independent of how the service provider intended for the space to be used. These emotional designations can be used to understand how the user sees a service and the role it plays in their life.[22]

Because library users are complex people with varying experiences, expectations, and needs, our role in a user-centered environment is to understand the user well enough to be able to meet or exceed their expectations by creating experiences that correspond to their needs. While the complexity of the user plays a key role in how we design our services, we also have to work with the physical, operational, and cultural environment that we inherit as employees to adjust and adapt it to current user needs and expectations.

ADAPTING THE INHERITED ECOLOGY

Rarely do we get the chance to create our own library from the ground up. As funding permits, libraries build new additions, become rehoused in new buildings, or reinvent themselves by adopting the latest and greatest trends. Regardless of how the library renovates, the same people in the same departments usually end up running the same services, just in a new location. How do we become more user-centered in these well-formed environments?

Libraries, like most organizations, are *inherited ecologies*[23] that, throughout time, create their own rich behavior. They are complex spaces where culturally specific rituals[24] are conducted and mature behaviors develop. They are "ecologies with the attendant constraints, expectations, and rituals,"[25] and deeply ingrained methods and processes. These qualities infuse and percolate throughout the organizational culture to influence the service provider and the user's experience. As new staff are hired, these rituals and behaviors are then inherited and imposed on newer staff.

The inherited ecology not only refers to the physical elements—such as an oversized reference desk that is more a part of the building than the service delivery proposition or a planned help desk that was reinvented as a print station—but also methods and processes. When considering new services or rethinking current service delivery models, librarians must consider three aspects of the ecology that might need reshaping or reenvisioning: physical, operational, and cultural. Physical is obvious; it relates to physical elements in the library ecology. Sometimes a desk needs to be moved or new signage needs to be added to help people find their way around the building. Operational involves rethinking how a service might be performed or delivered. It includes the intangible aspects or mechanics of how we deliver services. As new methods and techniques related to technology become commonplace, operational methods change to adapt to those new tools.

The biggest barrier to any type of change is cultural. Changing culture takes time, effort, and a willingness on the part of staff to shift how they do things, and change is not always accepted. Morville wrote, "[T]he biggest barriers in user experience aren't design and technology but culture and governance."[26] Ideas about how to conduct our business have become embedded in the library staff collective consciousness. When discussing or introducing newer services, how often have you heard, "That's how we've always done it"? The inherited ecology is about how current library staff (and users) accept the current culture. That culture could have been created long before any of the current services were in place. It may have made sense when there were card catalogs, but now that there are responsive design online catalogs, it may be necessary to rethink how we talk about how users find books and wayfind in the library.

Library departments were created around task fulfillment and managing what is "ours," without looking at the greater context or how services are actually being consumed. It might be time to reconsider the inherited ecology as it pertains to staff. The flipside of this is that we place the same cultural imposition on our users. The inherited ecology and culture of "that's how we've always done it" dictates that users conform to our methods rather than the library evolving to changing user behavior. Without thinking about how we can adapt the inherited ecology to our current users, we reinforce the idea that they have to adapt to work within our system, requiring every new user to pass through a rite of passage of sorts to understand how we operate.

Entering a new ecology requires a sort of rite of passage. There are three phases to any passage: separation, transition, and incorporation.[27] Our focus is on the transition or liminal phase when users are what Turner refers to as "betwixt and between."[28] During the liminal phase, users are between ecologies in a cultural limbo[29] prior to being incorporated into a new ecology. It is at this point when we, as the purveyors of that new ecology, impresses upon new users our methods for interacting with our inherited systems and ecology.

When new users enter our library ecology, we expect them to act a certain way. We create signs and post instructions reminding them how to behave and use our services. Sometimes this is necessary because of fixed systems that are not as malleable as they should be, but we also do this when it is not necessary because our internal culture dictates that users interact with our systems in a certain way. We impress upon our users the need to enter into a rite of passage.[30] As new users separate themselves from their previous library, they enter a liminal or transitional period[31] in the new library ecology. During this phase, we educate them as best we can with signage, online resource guides, and pamphlets. After a period of time, users become familiar with how things work and may be reincorporated as an expert user of the library system. As newer users enter our ecology and as expectations and technology change, rather than showing or dictating how to use older systems, perhaps we need to begin asking our users, "So, how do you work?" or "How do you want to work?"

EVERYTHING IS A SERVICE

When we look closely at how people utilize library spaces, it becomes increasingly clear that all library offerings are services, including those things that are often overlooked, furniture and collections. When users "hire" a piece of the library's physical infrastructure, (e.g., table, chair, desk, computer) to help them complete a task, they are using it as a service. As such, everything that a library has to offer is a service. Tables, chairs, printing, computing, and reference and circulation desks are all services. By looking at these offerings in this way, it is easier to see how users actually use the space, adapt it to meet their needs, and see ways to improve their experience.

As service providers, librarians are responsible for checking in periodically with their users to better understand expectations. As users change, so do expectations and the idea of "normal." Library staff should check in from time to time to ensure that current services, (e.g., chairs, tables, circulation, computing, reference), are delivering on their promise. Are they meeting user needs? If not, what are the current needs of users? How can we meet or exceed current needs to deliver on that original promise of the service? By thinking about these questions in the context of the service proposition, you can begin to collect the various pieces of evidence that illustrate the user's experience. These pieces of evidence help to create a picture of who our users are and what they need from you.

THE POWER OF CONFIRMATION

Through research and collecting evidence, librarians will begin to understand and confirm what users do in a library space and what they might need from it. The purpose of research is to "see how something exists, how it is embedded in a context of the relationships and associations, [so] we [can] begin to understand it."[32] Staff anecdotes and memories can inform this research, but should not be the basis for modeling service delivery. Creating an excellent user experience stems from finding the evidence behind actions rather than basing service creation on someone's memory. As we begin to better understand, we can solve the existing problems. By using various tools of inquiry from the service design toolkit, the research team can compile a body of data that can be used to define problems and develop solutions.

In service design, confirmation is used to make the intangible tangible. The goal is to bring to the surface the elements that make a service a service or the infrastructure function like a service. Using tools, such as ethnography, customer journey mapping, blueprinting, and journaling (to name a few), we can begin to piece together the overall user experience and identifying users' methods for interacting with the library infrastructure and touchpoints. How do they find a book? How do they find their way around the library? How do they use this table? Is this a table for reading, writing, computing, or organizing their notes for that personal family-tree project or paper assignment? Are the comfortable chairs used for reading or napping (or both)? The intent of confirmation is to make the evidence of how resources are used tangible.

SCALABILITY AND TIME

Service design is a scalable methodology. Its tools and methods employed can be constructed to fit whatever is being measured. Service design is flexible and malleable enough to be used on a wide range of projects, including finding out more about how books are circulated, to looking at how a specific space is used, to discovering how users feel about reference services, to comprehensively reviewing every service point in the library, to preparing for a large-scale renovation. It can scale between projects that are small in scope to those large in scope.

Finding time to evaluate services is always a challenge, especially if there are no complaints. We tend to want solutions to remedy our current problems. While we encourage libraries to think about evaluating and assessing services regardless of whether there is a perceived issue or problem, the reality is that there may only be time to complete a small-scale project. When this is the case, focusing on a known issue can be a good place to start. In addition to being scalable to fit any size project, service design can also accommodate any budgeted time allotment. When conducting a service design project, the research team will move the project through phases using tools and activities geared toward the appropriate phases. There is no duration requirement for a phase or tool. This book highlights the various phases and tools but does not give defined parameters related to duration. Essentially, when you're done, you're done.

In our space-usage analysis at Reed College Library, it took our Library User Experience group (LUX) two-plus years to complete our research efforts. This was the result of not having anyone working full-time on the project. Serving on the LUX was only one part of each member of our team's jobs. Service design allows the research team to work flexibly.

SUMMARY

- Libraries are tightly coupled, complex systems composed of many smaller systems. Throughout the years, library organizations have been divided by task and function, and have lost their systems view of operations. As a result of these silos, librarians have lost a sense of the bigger picture when planning or conducting assessment, focusing on the immediate rather than the holistic.
- From the user's perspective, everyone who works in a library is a librarian. The user doesn't see the library as a series of departments broken down by task or function. They come to the library with the intention of fulfilling a personal task. They also have expectations based on perceived similar services. When the library doesn't meet those expectations, the user may opt to find a substitute. From the user's perspective, the library is a whole rather than a series of departments.
- Libraries are inherited ecologies. Librarians inherit the building and the library presence from their predecessors. Without thinking, we tend to perpetuate the library culture we inherit. When we rethink services, we need to reconsider the current inherited ecology to determine what does and does not work. Systems created when the library was first built might not work for present users.
- Everything is a service. As we begin to look closer at how users actually utilize library spaces and resources, we can see that they use things as services. Desks, tables, and chairs, along with books and databases, are services they "hire" to help them fulfill personal tasks or assignments.
- Service design is a highly functional assessment method. But it shines when we look at how well it scales. Service design can help you look at how something as large as an entire building or as small individual chairs are used. You can use it to look at staffed service points and service delivery, as well as how common spaces like lobbies are used. Service design is malleable and scalable, and will work in any library environment.

Chapter Two

What Is Service Design

THE EVOLUTION OF SERVICES

There have always been services, although their value has not always been understood and appreciated. In 1776, Adam Smith took a systemic view in *The Wealth of Nations*, which created the foundation of modern capitalism. He wrote about all aspects of society in his description of the nature of commerce and specified two types of labor: productive and unproductive. He believed services were unproductive labor and a necessary evil[1] in the age of manufacturing. Compared to manufacturing labor, the "labour of a menial servant, on the contrary, adds to the value of nothing."[2] Smith based his negative view of services on the then-commonly held belief that without pecuniary return on investment, services and "menial servants" cost more than the value returned. He added sovereigns, soldiers, and statesmen, as well as "churchmen, lawyers, physicians, men of letters of all kinds; players, buffoons,[3] musicians, opera-singers, opera-dancers, &c."[4] to his list of occupations that didn't add value to society.

But times have changed, and in the 200-plus years since *The Wealth of Nations* was published, manufacturing has been replaced by a service-based economy. Services now account for more than 77 percent of the U.S. gross domestic product (GDP).[5] So while buffoons may still be buffoons, we now place a higher value on services than Smith did in 1776. Despite the low value he placed on services, Smith demonstrated an understanding of the service offering. In his critique, he states, "[S]ervices generally perish in the very instant of their performance, and seldom leave any trace or value behind them."[6] While the concept of lingering *value* can be disputed, the *trace* Smith refers to is the experience that lingers with the user. What remains from any service encounter is the residue of experience. To design excellent services, service providers must create positive user experiences. In this chapter, we review what makes something a service, the types of services offered by libraries, and how service adds value for users. We also discuss the characteristics of optimal experiences, including how to create an experience for your users.

WHAT IS A SERVICE?

Services are these intangible exchanges that cannot be possessed[7] and can only be "experienced, created, or participated in."[8]

Types of Services: Library Core Service Categories

Services can generally be classified in three categories: *care* (e.g., health care, accountants, mechanics); *access* (e.g., librarians, teachers, transportation, utilities); and *response* (e.g., first responders, waiters).[9] Depending on how a service is consumed, there is usually overlap in these categories. Libraries have similar core service categories that typically fall into one of two groups: *access to information* and *enabling task fulfillment*.

Access to information describes dynamic services that elicit a response based on a user's expressed need or request for something. These services get our users in touch with information and include help from librarians and paraprofessionals, information from the library or other websites, articles and other sources provided by databases, general reference assistance, circulation services, and interlibrary loans and document delivery. Services that enable task fulfillment are nondynamic and include such items as tables, chairs, desks, couches, computers,[10] printers, and scanners/copiers. These are often overlooked when we think about services, but they are important to consider because they enable users to perform and fulfill tasks.

The library space, or servicescape,[11] includes the classifications of dynamic and nondynamic services. It is the context or backdrop where all other services happen, and it plays an important role in how we perform services and how they are experienced by users. Measuring, managing, and nurturing the physical space is essential for optimal service delivery and user experience.

These core service categories are commonly used library services, but they also represent user expectations. For example, a chair in a library may help a user read a book; a table may help them write a paper or organize a family tree by providing space to spread out; and a reference librarian may help them find U.S. GDP data for the last 30 years, or maybe answer the question, "How many electoral college votes did Teddy Roosevelt receive in the 1904 election?"[12] In these examples, the various services, be they dynamic or nondynamic, offer access to information and the ability to fulfill personal tasks. The library is a complex system with services scattered throughout the environment. Users have expectations for how services should work to fulfill their needs, and as service providers, library staff must measure, assess, and manage them to meet or exceed expectations.

Anatomy of a Service

Services are composed of a few basic components: *context, purpose and function, interaction, inability to be possessed,* and *time.* While not all components are necessary, the majority will be present in any service. Figure 2.1 is an example of a service. A student is using a table to spread out his notebooks, computer, and other school-related items. Working at a table in the library is the context. The purpose and function of the table are for studying. The student doesn't own the table or the space. He is only using them for the time he has allotted for this task and no more. And the only thing he takes with him from using this service (aside from his completed homework assignment) is his experience of using this table in this area of the library.

Context

Services are contextual and should be designed for a specific environment. That place, or servicescape, influences user behavior when interacting with the service but also plays a role in how the service is delivered. [13] The context impacts the experience and can influence both the service provider and the user. It provides the backdrop for the service and should be taken into consideration as services are created or refined. While two distinct libraries may offer similar services, the different contexts of the libraries will influence how the service is delivered by staff and received by users.

Purpose and Function

Services have purpose. They don't exist for their own sake, but to perform a function related to a real or perceived need. Thinking about the purpose of the service can help determine if it is meeting current needs. For example, a major library service is space, which is filled with chairs and tables. The purpose of this service is to provide different types of seating and surfaces for users to complete tasks. Being aware of the types of tasks that users want to do should drive the type of tables available and how they are configured in the space. If you know users want to do mostly group work, it does not make sense to fill the library with individual study carrels.

Figure 2.1.   A student using a library table as a service to complete a homework assignment.

Interaction

Services require interactions between providers and users. For the library, this usually involves a librarian or paraprofessional playing the service provider role and a library patron receiving the service. But not all interactions require two humans; they can also occur between a human and some technological interface or with a physical object in a space. In all instances, an interaction will involve two parties where at least one party experiences the exchange.

The Inability to Be Possessed

Services cannot be possessed, only experienced. While a service exchange may involve two parties, neither party owns it. The experience is intangible and cannot be seen. When users take advantage of services, they don't own anything tangible when the interaction ends. A person who eats dinner at a nice restaurant will leave with a full belly, but they won't possess anything touchable when the experience ends. They enjoyed being waited on and not having to worry about clearing the table or washing dishes and are left with only a memory. "Each experience derives from the interaction between the staged event,"[14] so users leave with only memories, which create or reinforce their opinions of the service and may either persuade or dissuade them from entering into an exchange with that service again.

Time

Services take time to perform and complete. The research team should consider time as an important element in the design of services, including thinking about how time can be manipulated and feedback mechanisms inserted into the process to inform users about their progression toward task completion. This makes time not only a characteristic of a service, but also a tool. While we do not recommend entering the world of Taylorism and ruling the library and its services by the ticking hands of a clock, the research team needs to be mindful of how time impacts experiences[15] and at what point users give up and resign themselves to feelings of dissatisfaction.

There are two types of time: *journey time* and *provider time*. Journey time is the amount of time it takes a user to complete a task. It is completely arbitrary and depends on the user's moods, focus, and various other facets of the customer journey. Provider time is the amount of time generally required for the provider to fulfill a task. When thinking about time in relation to a specific service, the research team should consider both sides of the service exchange and the following questions: How long will it take for a user to complete a task? At what point is an exchange complete? What is a reasonable time expectation for the service? When should the provider inform the user of any delays in the system? From the provider's side, how long is too long to work on a task before requesting additional assistance or notifying someone that a problem exists?

TYPES OF EXPERIENCE

When talking about experiences, it is important to clarify who is doing the experiencing. Service design asks the research team to view services holistically by looking at the *user experience* and *service provider experience*.

User experience refers to the user or patron's experience with a service. The most common usage of "user experience" refers to the user interacting with technology or a computer interface. We expand on this definition to encompass the user experience with the technology, but also all aspects of the library. Essentially, we argue that the user experience is the "sum of the task experiences involved in using a service."[16] It is task-oriented and includes experiences with both physical and virtual resources, but it does not include library staff, unless they are using the library in a nonworking capacity.

Service provider experience refers to the library staff experience when performing a service. It includes all offstage and onstage activities from the service provider's perspective. Since services are a co-production between the service provider and the user, offstage time is equally important to on-stage time. The literal egress of a service provider from one stage may actually be an entrance to another stage where they may be a user and a provider.[17]

CREATING THE EXPERIENCE

No two users have the same experience.[18] Put two people in the same room and one will be colder than the other. One will think the lighting is not as bright. One may take issue with the paint. We have different experiences in shared environments, but by using evidence from research, libraries can create user-centered environments that appeal to the constituents we serve. By having users inform us about the experiences we have created and working to create the types of experiences they desire, we can design delightful services.

Staging the experience is key to how it will be perceived. While service providers can never satisfy every user, by understanding who our users are, we can attempt to meet or exceed expectations by setting them up to have a good experience. So, what do we mean by an experience? "[It] is a cover-all term . . . through which a person knows and constructs a reality."[19] It is the combination of feelings and emotions tied to an event within a given context. As humans, we create experiences every day. Our sensory organs are constantly receiving information and signals from the surrounding environment. As a result, we begin to associate feelings and emotions with different contexts and environments. Imagine going to the gym and having a great workout. Upon leaving the workout room, you get a whiff of buttered popcorn from the check-in desk. The feeling of physical exertion and the smell of the popcorn may remind you of the gym and the good experience you had there. But when you return the following week and can't get good momentum or break a sweat, the previous good experience is influenced by a feeling of not having done enough on the elliptical machine. Maybe that popcorn scent doesn't help, either.

Now imagine that your car has been shaking a bit when you apply the brakes and you need to have the brakes looked at. You take it to a local brake shop, and the mechanic tells you there's nothing major wrong. The rotors may need to be adjusted, but it won't take more than an hour. The only service he is selling is the adjustment of the rotors, nothing else. So you grab a bag of free popcorn, sit, and read that book you've been carrying around but haven't had a chance to open. You feel good. An hour later, you are fine with paying for the brake adjustment because the staff were honest, didn't try to upsell you on anything, and gave you a bag of popcorn to keep you occupied while you waited. That brake shop is now associated with a good experience.

Given the fact that experiences are unique to each user and based on their interpretation of events, can we even design an experience? After all, the experience is created in the mind of the user at the point of contact with a touchpoint. In short, no, we cannot design an exact experience. There are too many user-specific feelings or emotions we cannot control. But we can attempt to remove known barriers that prevent a positive experience. If we are successful at eliminating known barriers, we can set the stage for a good user experience.

Audience

The people in our audience are our users. This may include moms, dads, children, students, professors, professional staff, judges, elected officials, or anyone who uses the library. They are the people we design for and with. [20] When considering how they use the library and what they expect from it, "we need to think in terms of designing for relationships and experiences that evolve and change over time, rather than just in terms of short moments of consumption or usage." [21] The act of designing a service with users is essentially about creating a long-term relationship between user, service provider, and the ecology. Services should meet or exceed current user needs and also accommodate future users. As an audience of users grows or moves on, you should keep meeting with them to continually learn changing habits and needs.

Knowing your audience and users is the first step in creating the optimal experience. "[T]he more generic the person for whom the designer is designing, the less likely the experience will be exciting, memorable, or unique." [22] Without an idea of who they are, we can't possibly believe that we can design for them. The traditional quantitative approach, which only tells you gross usage and a employs a qualitative approach to get those deeper insights, will reveal who your users are and what motivates them. Only through a hands-on approach can you begin to understand the various members of your audience and actual users of the library's resources.

Experience as Performance

Our role in creating the experience is managing the parts we can control. We can control the temperature, lighting, service providers (to a certain extent), and overall appearance of the environment. If the user enters the library having just lost their job or received a poor grade on a test, their experience of the space will be influenced by the previous event. Our role in creating the service experience is to diffuse (or infuse) any user experience with a positive experience of the library through professional behavior, responsive and efficient workflows, and a pleasant environment.

As we look at creating the experience, we must look at the user and the space, and design experiences that support the rituals that happen there.[23] Responding to rituals, behavior, and expectations are fundamental in creating the user experience. The types of interactions that happen in the library are situation specific. As Max Weber once said, "Events are not just there and happen, but they have a meaning and happen because of that meaning." Through researching user behavior and expectations, we can understand the meaning behind what Weber was talking about and design a functional space that accommodates current user needs and desires. Interactions don't happen in a vacuum, they happen in a context rich with its own culture and behaviors.[24] Thus, the technology and furniture in a space should cater to the rituals and behaviors that take place there. Libraries must design for the "jobs to be done," as users see it, not just how we want it to be.

Pine and Gilmore equate designing the experience with a form of theater, complete with onstage and offstage areas.[25] To create the stage and the experience, consider three aspects of staging the experience: *scripting*, *context*, and *wayfinding*.

Scripting

Scripting is the choreography of the physical service. It can be broken down further into three categories: *sequence*, *progression*, and *duration*.[26] Sequencing is the order in which things happen, starting with considering when the service encounter begins. Does it begin when the user enters the front door or only after they have spoken to someone at a service desk? Does it include making eye contact or verbally greeting the user? To design an experience, a set sequence of tasks should be choreographed by the design team. For example, Starbucks did this when they set up the flow of their ordering and pickup lines, and it is one of the reasons they are so successful. Customers know what they are likely to experience when they stop in for a cup of coffee because the process has been carefully scripted, to include sequencing where they go first when entering the store, how they are going to be greeted, what they will be asked, what the person behind the counter does after hearing the order, how they will pay, and how they will pick up their order.

Progression is the momentum that builds up as the user flows through the environment. It includes attending to how users move through the steps to complete tasks. Are there any impediments to the flow of completing a task? If so, are they necessary (e.g., a loadbearing wall might be a necessary impediment or the location of a stairwell or elevator to gain access to different floors)? If not, how can they be changed or how can the user be redirected to avoid them? In addition to thinking about impediments to flow, you should also think about how users experience the sequence and how it builds for them in a positive or negative way.

Going back to the Starbucks example, customers know that part of the Starbucks experience should include happy faces greeting them when they place their order and then again when they pick it up. In addition, the process ends with a reward: your favorite caffeinated beverage. In sum, the sequence progresses as scripted, building to the climactic moment of receiving something positive.

The last part of scripting is duration, which involves managing how long it will take different users to complete a task in a variety of conditions. Duration can make or break an experience. If the task is retrieving a book from the stacks, how long does it take a person who can walk versus a person in a wheelchair or on crutches? How will that influence duration? When they arrive at the circulation desk, how long will it take for them to check out the book? If there is a line, is there a feedback mechanism in place to provide them with estimated wait times? Unfortunately, life does not come equipped with a built-in progress bar (see figure 2.2), so we have to provide the user with feedback on their progress or when part of the service is missing or not performing as designed. Knowing or understanding the various barriers that exist in scripting, progression, and duration provides librarians with the information to remove any friction to make the overall experience more pleasurable. [27]

Context as Setting

"Ambience is the proverbial 'secret sauce' to any . . . memorable interaction." [28] Next to the collection, the library's most valuable asset is its physical space. When setting the stage for service delivery, the primary actor in the drama is the physical space or "servicescape." [29] The physical space has the "capacity to determine the way in which its occupants see the world." [30] The servicescape impacts both users and service providers, and includes every surface, floor space, chair, table, and stair. [31] Its collection of "atmospherics" [32] provide the backdrop for experiences. They are the physical cues [33] in any environment, for instance, smells, temperatures, colors, decor, textures, and overall physical appearance of a space or resource. The atmospherics also play a role in how the user adapts the environment to their needs. In talking about the ghats at Benares, Lyndon writes, "Every step is a potential place." [34] Similar to every step being a potential place, the library is full of potential places.

Figure 2.2.   Life does not come with a progress bar. Providing a feedback mechanism where possible will help the patron know how long they have to wait.

Users see more than just tables and chairs when they enter the library; they see places that can be adapted to suit their requirements. Essentially, they see opportunities. Figure 2.3 shows two young library users at a table. One is working on his homework, while the other is turning a surface into a place to sit. Something we've noticed in our own work is that students adapt flat surfaces so they can stand up and study. When you look at the library through the eyes, questions about seemingly mundane things like the cleanliness of the tables, the number of outlets, and the ease of furniture movement take on more importance. These small details lead to the overall impression of a space and heavily influence the user experience.

Wayfinding

Being able to navigate the physical or virtual space of a library is essential. Library users rarely navigate one environment without consulting the other. Not only is it necessary for them to be able to get from point A to point C via point B, but a coherent design and layout should also be mirrored between the physical and virtual. The website is the library's other front door—one that is open 24 hours a day. In recent years, libraries have emphasized the

Figure 2.3. Two young library patrons using a table to suit their needs.

usability of website user interfaces, but it is essential to include the physical layout of the library as well, since users see the virtual library and the physical library as a single entity. Our job is to make their experience seamless[35] and easy to navigate.

When looking at wayfinding, ask some of the following questions: Do the ideas and labels on hyperlinked items make sense? Are the naming conventions on the web the same used verbally at all touchpoints? Are the physical library spaces named the same as on the map on the website? Krug gives three reasons for wayfinding: "It tells us what's here, it tells us how to use the site, and it gives us confidence in the people who built it."[36] Navigation, both in person and on the web, shouldn't require too much thinking. It should help the immediate environment make sense and not distract from completing tasks.

Consistency

The user experience rarely happens through a single channel.[37] Libraries are highly integrated systems consisting of physical (e.g., the physical library, reference and circulation desks) and virtual (e.g., library website, chat service, e-mail) channels. Due to the increasing levels of complexity in both types of spaces, users typically have to navigate both to get to what they need. Consistency in labeling and naming conventions used on the website, at the circulation and reference desks, in the printed literature and on wall maps, and in the physical library is integral to creating a unified and optimal user experience. Using colloquial naming conventions might throw some users off and negatively influence their overall experience.

Designing the Complete Experience

Designing the overall experience requires a holistic view of the library. All of the touchpoints in the library interact and are interdependent. For example, a wall map exists to reinforce and guide the user through the physical library, the website is the portal to finding items in the collection or a librarian for help, and the physical space is a storehouse of books and a space with tables and chairs. Together, these items make up the library. As stewards of the library, we are responsible for providing optimal user experiences that change and adapt as expectations evolve. Considering that the library delivers a complete experience—and not a small series of interactions with separate library departments—it is clear that a powerful method for measuring, creating, and refining services is essential. While there are many different methods to choose from, the strength of service design is that it looks at the service delivery model holistically and evaluates experiences with actual users to refine, adapt, or create new services.

SERVICE DESIGN: A DEFINITION

"Service design is a holistic, co-creative, and user-centered approach to understanding customer behavior for the creation or refining of services."[38] It involves working closely with users, both internal and external, to define problems and solutions. With service design, all aspects of the library are considered a service and looked at holistically, which allows us to see how integrated the different parts of the experience are and how each individual element can be adapted to influence the overall experience. Solutions may be large or small, as long as they improve the user experience. Adopting a service design mindset includes looking at the bigger picture and the role of services in the library, as well as who is responsible for each of the moving parts. Service design encourages us to put away our blinders and look beyond the silos and artificial divisions created within the library. In the following chapters, we explore the service design mindset and tools.

The Family of Designs

In recent years, there has been an increasing interest in using qualitative research methods in libraries. With the advent of the Internet, libraries have increasingly focused on delivering services via electronic interface, studying the user experience, and delivering services in response to user behavior. Qualitative methods like ethnography, interviewing, and observation are now commonplace in libraries. One method that has been adopted by many libraries is participatory design. While relatively new in the library environment, participatory design has its roots in Scandinavia dating to the 1970s,[39] with the introduction of technology in the workplace.[40] In participatory design, users are asked early on to participate in the process of creating spaces or web interfaces that more closely meet their needs. Service design also shares characteristics with interface design in that the design of a service is merely the design of an interface, but on a three-dimensional scale.

While similar tools are employed in other methods, the emphasis in service design is on "functionality and form of services"[41] within a unique environment. It "differs in that it emphasizes the entire ecology in the delivery of service."[42] Service design requires collaborating with actual users to co-create solution by looking at the entire ecology using a systems thinking and user-centered approach to better inform the fit and function of services.

THE SERVICE DESIGN MINDSET

First and foremost, service design is a mindset[43] researchers and others can adopt to help them better understand how users perceive services. It requires that researchers break out of their usual mode of thinking to see services with a fresh eye and a new perspective on user needs and expectations. Approaching any research problem with an open mind and a willingness to learn and see the larger picture opens up possibilities to evolve and learn with users. Service design is more than just implementing a few tools, gathering insights, and synthesizing the data. It requires that you alter your perspective and embrace empathy in order to get closer to users and an authentic understanding of their perspective on the library and its services.

Service design includes a robust set of tools. Some tools (such as design ethnography) have a foundation in traditional anthropological methods. Other tools (customer journey mapping, blueprinting, and prototyping) draw from the user experience professional's toolkit to help with visualizing the steps required to perform a task. It also includes more traditional tools (like journaling) to help us better understand users in their own words. Finally, it draws from the performing arts by using scenarios to help stage a scene to get a reaction and plan for the actual performance of services.

With a fresh perspective and a series of tools, we are ready to approach the research challenges that lay ahead. Let's take a closer look at the mindset required for service design.

ELEMENTS OF THE SERVICE DESIGN MINDSET

Co-Creating

Service exchanges are co-productions. When a provider and a user of a service interact to complete a task, they have co-produced an experience and performed something akin to a piece of theater. In service design, we measure and observe current exchanges and work closely with current internal and external stakeholders to co-design services. Co-creation happens when service providers and users work together to better understand needs and expectations[44] to refine, revise, or create new services.

In any service design project, the research team will work closely with a group of users on a variety of exercises and in discussion sessions to uncover motivations and expectations behind user actions. Co-creation is not limited to testing actual users; it is a necessary mindset of service design because it requires the research team to trust that the user knows best how they want services delivered. We must view services through their eyes, which can only be done by working closely with them to determine which services should be offered and how we should offer them.

Making the Intangible Tangible

Service design "deconstruct[s] service processes into single touchpoints and interactions."[45] In doing so, the research team can identify the various tasks, departments, choices, feelings, and internal and external processes involved in the completion of a task. Services normally involve a request and an exchange, which can be verbal or physical, followed by the production of evidence. For example, a receipt or e-mail documenting that a transaction occurred may provide evidence of the transaction. While the request and exchange are not invisible, most of the steps involved happen in the user's mind as they journey to complete a task. Analyzing the user journey to find the intangible steps and then making them visible provides a picture of how truly integrated the library is.

We can make the invisible steps tangible by creating such dynamic visualizations as a customer journey map or blueprint, or through staging scenarios. Another reason to make tasks tangible is to pinpoint and investigate touchpoints, which "occur any time a user uses or interacts with your product or service."[46] Examples include the website, help desks, tables and chairs, virtual chat, e-mail, public computers, and so on. Identifying touchpoints and the steps involved in completing a process can help you identify potential trouble spots.

Confirming with Evidence

Too often in librarianship we base our decisions on our own biases and assumptions about users.[47] Adopting the mindset and using the tools of service design provides a powerful method for either confirming or disabusing notions you may have of your users. Gathering evidence and insights to inform decision-making ensures that services fit with not only what users say they want, but also what they actually do.

Another common decision-making error is relying on national trends or returning from a conference and basing decisions on what worked in a different library. It is important to keep up to date on trends and library literature, but outside trends should always be only one part of the internal decision-making process. Because each library is a unique ecology with its own set of users set within a larger environment (city, state, college, university, etc.), user behavior has to be studied and understood for that specific place. While ideas from other libraries may inspire you, it is important to make sure those ideas are a good fit for your user group.

Focusing on User Needs and Expectations

At its heart, librarianship is a service industry dedicated to serving users. The focus of service design is on user needs, but also user expectations. User expectations are based on previous experiences with similar services[48] that they've encountered in their daily lives. People tend to group or cluster similar experiences together to form an internal expectation.[49] Understanding how and what people think about your services and where they see similarities with other services can help you understand current needs and expectations.

A common example is the functionality of websites. Using websites to find people, things, and services has become daily practice for most Americans. Because users understand the basics of how websites should function, they can get frustrated when one does not meet their expectations. If menus don't work the way they do on other sites or if the site is too slow or cluttered, they may suspect something is broken or think poorly of the library. A common and related example from academic libraries is how difficult it is for many students and faculty to maneuver from article citations indexed in the catalog or a database to the full text of the article in another database. This process usually takes several clicks, leaving users with the perception that it is easier to use Google Scholar and other sources on the open web because the full text is either there or it's not. While librarians know that subscription databases and open web sources are not the same, users don't understand the difference, so they assign a value based on what they perceive as a less positive experience.

In the first example, the library is in a position to meet expectations by improving the website. The second example is more complicated because we often have little control about how the databases work and interact with one another, but one solution might be to give feedback on the steps as the user proceeds through them. While we can't always meet expectations due to outside factors, we can adapt the system to make the process less onerous or provide clear communication about it.

Thinking Holistically

Thinking holistically is the ability to see the highly integrated and coupled library system for what it is. The library is a group of tightly coupled systems working together to perform services. To operate holistically, it is important to keep the bigger picture in mind when designing services. While it might be impossible to think of every single aspect of a service, the research team has to strive toward that goal by considering the larger context and ecology in which a service exists and operates.[50] Knowing the impact that changes to a service can have on both user and staff provider experience is important. When we think holistically, we quickly realize that "each and every action contributes to the total experience,"[51] and as von Humboldt realized when looking at nature, "no single fact can be considered in isolation."[52] What works for the natural world works for the built environment.

Having Empathy

The goal of empathy is to "feel what it's like to be another person" through "acquiring [the] feelings"[53] of another person. Employing empathy allows us to "observe the world in minute detail,"[54] but efforts to do so may be nearly impossible, because who can actually feel like someone they aren't? At the very least, by adopting an empathetic mindset when studying and designing services, we can approximate a user's world[55] to "see the world as [they] do."[56] Tripp observed that, "with empathy, you can start with what's needed by your customers and figure out a way to serve them."[57]

The service design process puts the user in the center and works outward from there. Without a sense of empathy with their journey and behavior, we could never learn what we might be doing wrong or how to better meet their expectations and needs. It is crucial to take care of all aspects of the experience, or "there is a danger that many parts of the service experience will 'just happen' . . . [and] this isn't good enough."[58] Using empathy will help you remember the purpose of the service design project and get you to think outside of your box and attend to all parts of the user's experience. While empathy is a well-known tool for service design veterans, it takes a great deal of effort to care about the actual user journey and understand the hurdles they face. Remembering to care and empathize is key to any team's efforts.

Being Open-minded and Not a Devil's Advocate

Service design is an exploratory process that requires participating members to have an open mind and a willingness to learn. To have a truly open mind, the research team should be optimistic about the project and feel that what they are doing will lead to important new insights and improved services that will add value to the library. As part of the service design process, you will work closely with a user working group and other library colleagues. It is important that the process does not get bogged down with negativity or that ideas don't get shot down with that ubiquitous statement "we've tried that before."

It is essential to create a safe space for everyone involved with your service design project, that includes both staff and user participants. The best ideas are often borne from ideas that may sound crazy at first. Invoking the devil's advocate can be the death knell of innovation because it shoots people and ideas down too early in the process. While the devil's advocate can be a powerful analytical tool, it is too often used to ridicule and belittle new ideas. When playing the devil's advocate, the speaker gets to hide behind a shield of negativity and essentially dismantle ideas before they have a chance to be fully vetted, considered, and confirmed, or disconfirmed with evidence. Focusing on problems too early in the process can hinder any possible innovation.[59] Our goal in service design is not only to understand how services are used, but also to create new services or refine current ones. We can only do that by confirming with evidence and looking at all possibilities for solutions, no matter how crazy they may seem at first. To make service design work, the team needs to trust the process and the insights gathered by observing and interacting with actual users, and that other members are willing to learn and be open to new ideas. Great solutions come from allowing each idea their time in the sun. This is not to say that members of the research team can't disagree. By all means, have healthy discussions full of debate. But keep the devil's advocate out of early discussions. Let the evidence and insight talk. If you listen, you may hear a solution worth taking up.

Being Willing to Evolve

The line "I knew everything once and now I know it all again"[60] sums up a willingness to be wrong and a willingness to evolve and learn. Before starting any service design project, the research team has to feel comfortable with the idea of possibly being wrong. Being wrong is nothing to feel bad about.

On the contrary, it should be quite empowering because it demonstrates a willingness and ability to learn and truly be user-centered.

Going back to the idea of "knowing our users" can lead to trouble. It is easy to fall into the trap of thinking you can't be wrong if you believe you know your users and their behavior better than they know it themselves. This is what Madsbjerg and Rasmussen call "default thinking."[61] Allowing ourselves to be wrong and accepting that maybe we don't know everything is acceptable and an essential part of the process. And just like us, users are constantly evolving, becoming a bit of a moving target. In chapter 1, we discuss inherited ecology. While the library building may not change, it is the role and duty of the library staff to adapt the space and services to meet current needs and expectations.

Existing users may change because of new cultural norms or changing technology, or from moving into new life phases. We also gain new users from younger generations or different cultures. Both existing and new users bring their own beliefs and expectations with them, so what we once knew may no longer hold true, and things that used to work may no longer be functional. Responding to these changes provides opportunities to learn more about the people we serve and an avenue to finding new ways to deliver the value that only a library and a librarian can offer.

SUMMARY

- Services have evolved from being a necessary offshoot of production and industry to contributing to more than 77 percent of the U.S. GDP. As more developed nations change to service-based economies, more emphasis is being placed on the user (or customer) and their experience with goods and services.
- Services are intangible exchanges. Services cannot be owned, but they can be participated in and experienced. Services generally fall into three categories: care, access, and response. To further separate these categories, libraries offer two types of service within the general access category: access to information and enabling task fulfillment.
- Services are composed of several basic components: context (they happen somewhere and, as a result, certain behaviors are associated with them); purpose and function (they exist to help perform a function or fill a perceived need); interaction (they are exchanges between two or more parties); the inability to be possessed (they are created at the time of exchange and cannot be possessed by provider or user); and time (they take time and have duration).
- No two users experience the same service the same way. Experiences, unlike services, are possessed by the user. We can never totally control an

experience, but we can eliminate barriers to a positive experience. Part of creating the experience lies in creating the right "conditions,"[62] so services are tailored toward our specific audience(s), scripted to focused on the user, and constructed for the appropriate setting or context that works for a given experience. In short, we focus on the entire experience rather than just bits and pieces of an experience.

• Two types of experience that should be considered in any service design project are the user experience and the service provider experience. Service exchanges are co-produced at the point of exchange. Considering both user and service provider experience is important when developing solutions.

• Service design is a holistic, systems approach to service delivery assessment that is co-creative and user-centered. It is as much a mindset as it is a methodology that involves altering how we think about the service delivery model and how patrons expect to use and use our services.

Chapter Three

Service Design, in Practice

In this chapter, we focus on getting started with service design, along with breaking down the phases and providing details and the tools associated with each. It is important to note that what we are presenting here is a tool kit, not a prescribed set of steps. Service design is highly contextual, and its implementation should be based on and look different for each project. A project to redesign the reference area of a library should and will be different than a user study of digital collections, and both types of projects will vary by library.

In each section, we describe the purpose of the phase and cover key aspects that are important to be aware of when conducting a service design project. We also cover tools that can be used during certain phases. These are only suggestions, and teams should feel free to mix and match tools to gather the necessary data to move the project forward. These tools are discussed in greater detail in chapter 4.

PHASES OF SERVICE DESIGN

Prework Phase

The prework phase is about getting started. As the King of Hearts states in *Alice's Adventures in Wonderland*, "Begin at the beginning and go on until you end."[1] This phase focuses on project management and planning. While that may not appeal to everyone, it is a necessary step to get the project off to a good start. In this phase, you will create a research team, assign tasks and roles, devise team rules, define the scope of the project, build support from the library administration, and begin developing a timeline and schedule.

There are several steps you should take to get ready for your service design project. If you are setting up a research team to do several service design projects or a usability team that may use service design alone or with other user-study methods, you may only have to do some of these steps once and then just maintain your team. In this book, we call this team the *research team*.

Creating a Research Team

The research team will ultimately determine the success of your project, so you should think carefully about who will be on the team and what role each member will play. This may seem obvious, but it means thinking about both the functional expertise or official library role of the people involved and their softer skills, which may be less visible. For example, you will need people who are good at getting users involved with the library, someone with marketing and organizational acumen, someone experienced with or willing to learn about institutional review boards and ethical research practices, warm and open personalities that can get people talking in interviews and focus groups, analytical minds to break the data apart and look for different solutions, and at least one person willing to bring it all together in written reports and presentation materials.

You must also be sure that you have the appropriate functional expertise on your team. If you are planning a service design project for the entire library, it is crucial to have team members that can represent all of the library's functional areas. In turn, if your team plans to look at only one service, you need to be clear about how far that service reaches and make sure there is representation from all functional areas that feed into the service. Service design requires more involvement from stakeholders than many user-centered methodologies. Carefully involving stakeholders while designing the project and after getting initial results will address some of the necessary functional expertise. In fact, "service design can be described as the use of a designerly way of searching for solutions to problems in people-intensive service systems through the engagement of stakeholders."[2] While many methods use stakeholders at various points in the project, in service design, major stakeholders should be involved at all points in the evolution of the project, from inception to conclusion.

Think about designing a car.[3] When a team begins to design a car, they first need to share their vision of the type of car they are designing. If each member of the team begins with a different type of car in mind, they will approach the design with different—and often competing—ideas in mind. If one designer is thinking about an environmentally conscious hybrid, while another is imagining a giant SUV with all the trimmings, the two will clash before even getting started. This works the same way with functional expertise. Think about the following two scenarios:

1. Imagine you have already decided you are building an eco-friendly car, so you have that common goal worked out. Management has put together an "innovation team" that is working on designing, building, and selling the car, and includes people from all parts of the process. Everyone on the team works in a different area. One person on the team is a marketer, and they are thinking about how to sell the car, and another person is in charge of quality control and is envisioning the processes they need to ensure the car is built without any deficiencies. Your team will likely begin their work with the marketer thinking, "How soon can we get this car to market so we can start making money?" and the quality control expert thinking, "Great, how am I going to convince everyone on the team that high-quality products take time?" These two staff members (along with everyone else on the team) are working toward the common goal of building and selling an eco-friendly car, but they are approaching it from the perspective of their day-to-day work, which varies greatly between the two. Their vision of what they are building is the same, but their ideas for how to get there may be very different. Because of these differing viewpoints, they may also value different aspects of the design. For example, the marketer may be excited about highlighting a feature that those in manufacturing have deemed too time intensive to be worthwhile. The work of this team is messy and often takes a lot of time.

2. What if, instead, management put together an "innovation team" made up of only car designers and marketers, and no one focusing on the processes in between? Upper-level management decided that the rationale for this is that the innovative work being done is designing and marketing an eco-friendly car, and the processes in between will just follow the innovative ideas being handed down from the top. They have instructed the team to get input on the building process from manufacturing, on front-end selling from dealers, and on the driver experience from end users at "relevant" points in the process. The designers and the marketers are happy with this team because they are both focused on the end user experience. They want to make customers happy by producing an awesome car and believe that as long as they talk to the people actually building the car at some point during the manufacturing phase and to users once they have something ready to show them, their design process will have been inclusive. Upper-level management is especially happy with this approach because it appears to be efficient and considers user needs and opinions.

From a design perspective, is scenario 1 or 2 more ideal? Service design-ers would argue that even though scenario 1 may be messier and possibly take more time on the front end, it is the more ideal approach. Service design is about looking at the entire process, including all the little steps in between. Therefore, it is necessary to consider the work and perspectives of the people working on the in-between processes as being just as valid and important as the users and those working on the front end. As discussed in chapter 1, we have a tendency in libraries to separate and silo the work of access, technical, and public services. While library staff recognize some of the overlap in the work, it seldom comes into play in how we think about and design processes and services. The aforementioned scenarios highlight two points regarding putting together a good service design team.

1. You need functional expertise because you need the different perspec-tives on process to guide the design of services. Good services should make everyone happy, including the staff providing the service.
2. The differences in focus for the different team members mean you need to work quickly to develop your service concept (or purpose of the work) and the scope of your project.

Assigning Roles and Tasks

The research team has to perform certain types of tasks that require team members to take on various roles. Assigning roles at this stage can help the project gain momentum. The following roles and tasks are suggestions based on our own experience. We encourage library research teams to configure them as they see fit and in a way that allows for a high level of efficiency and camaraderie among team members.

The team may want to assign roles based on the level of comfort members have with one another and the duties assigned to each role. Depending on the size of the team, some members may have to take on multiple roles. For the purpose of this chapter, we describe the various roles needed on every ser-vice design project and assume that team size and makeup will depend on how your library creates project teams and allocates human resources.

Team Lead   The team lead is the team coordinator. This person acts as the main point of contact between the team and the library administration. He or she may also be the main provider of information shared with the rest of the library. While we encourage all members to take an active role in promot-ing the team's efforts, the occasional e-mail to the entire library may be necessary, and having those mass communications sent from a single person will help to establish a primary point of contact for library staff.

As the team coordinator, the team lead may also be in a position to recruit key members from the library staff to be part of the research team. We advise recruiting a core group of people to the research team. This will ensure continuity and a level of comfort among team members. There may be times when the team lead sees benefits to calling in a library staffer who holds some crucial piece of knowledge related to a project. If that is the case, recruiting that individual to help guide the team (without influencing the final outcome) can help move a project forward more quickly and comprehensively.

The team lead also manages project documentation. Documents needed may include timelines, project exercise descriptions and intended goals for performing these exercises, scope documents to make sure the project doesn't get out of hand, official communications to stakeholders, meeting minutes, and any final reports that may be required by library directors or other higher-ups.

Discussion Lead During discussion sessions with participants, it is best to have one person lead the discussion. While all members of the research team should actively participate, there should be a clear leader who begins and ends topics, and moves discussions along when meeting with the user working group (UWG) or other stakeholders. They may or may not play an active role in creating the questions, but they are the lead voice representing the library during discussion sessions. The purpose of a discussion lead is to give the UWG a single person to focus on and direct comments to. As clarification is required, additional members of the research team should speak up during the discussion sessions, but they should be mindful not to dominate the conversation, leaving most of the speaking to the participants. The discussion lead should concentrate on keeping the discussion moving and not take notes during the sessions.

Notetakers Documenting the process and meetings is important for later synthesis of the findings. Taking detailed notes during discussion sessions is a key role. We encourage having multiple people take notes because everyone does not hear the same thing during discussions. It can be helpful if all of the notetakers share their notes as soon as possible after the session has closed so everyone can review the discussion and find differences in understanding about any points covered. If the research team can afford to have three notetakers present and taking notes, the discussion process should be well covered. Having more than one notetaker ensures that key data and comments are captured.

Logistics Coordinator The logistics coordinator is in charge of preparing the setting for the discussion groups or various exercises. Are there enough whiteboards? Pencils? Notebooks? Pizza? Bubbly water? The logistics person takes care of these details. They book the room, make sure there are enough of the appropriate supplies for the given exercise, and get sustenance if you are feeding the participants.

Outreach Coordinator   No user-focused project can succeed without an outreach coordinator. To get feedback and data, you will need a group of participants willing to share their experiences. The outreach coordinator is in charge of getting the word out and finding ways to get users excited about participating in the project. There are users from every library who would love to share what they like and dislike, and are invested enough in the library to be committed to helping improve it. The outreach coordinator needs to find and attract those users. Outreach should be done in whatever way works for your community and usually needs to include more than one medium. You may choose to get the message out through posters and fliers, social media, e-mail, and/or an article in a student or community newspaper; by talking to regular users; or via any other methods you can think of.

The aforementioned tasks and roles play crucial parts in service design. Some teams may want to trade tasks as the team matures and proceeds through various projects, while others may want to stick with a given recipe due to different team members' skills and interests. The important thing is to find a structure that works for the team, stick with it, and document the process. Self-documentation should be reflexive and provide information for any newcomers to the team.

How Do We Get Library Staff to Think about Communication from the Student's Perspective?
By Vikram Chan-Herur

The Library User Experience (LUX) committee brainstormed ways to reach students for ideas and feedback, primarily through our focus groups. When I attend an event on campus, the following must happen first: I must learn that the event exists; decide that it is something worth considering attending; know when and where it will be held; determine whether I am free at that time; decide to attend; and, finally, attend. I used that as a framework for my thinking during the discussion. We identified several strategies likely to be useful for reaching students: electronic (direct e-mail and inclusion in a twice-weekly newsletter), physical (posters and mailings to student mailboxes), and talking to students individually.

To inform about the event and convince people that it was worth considering, we relied mostly on Reed students' attachment to specific library spaces, for example, "Rejuvenate the Reference Rooms?" "Optimize the Old Pit?" or "Perfect the Pollock Room?" Each approach used these headlines (except for talking in person). But we envisioned these various strategies having different strengths in the chain, from hearing about the focus group to attending. E-mail has the advantage of presenting information where it's easily used (i.e., on the same device as one's calendar); however, as a student, e-mail, both direct and in the campus newsletter, is easy to overlook. Both physical strategies are harder to miss. When I'm walking on campus, I see posters for events whether I want to or not, especially if they are strategically placed, in great enough quantity, and a nonstandard size or shape. Similarly, physical mailings are easy to encounter and require effort to ignore. For me, these physical strategies suffer the opposite problem of e-mail: They are harder to ignore but harder to act on, as my calendar is not as close to the information. Talking to students individually is inefficient and suffers the problems of both the physical and electronic methods, but it is often effective due to existing relationships.

Finally, to maximize the number of students who would be free at the time of the events and make it easy and appealing to attend, we scheduled them for the hour between when late afternoon classes get out and evening classes start—dinnertime for many—and offered food. This further minimized the effort required to attend; the event was basically time neutral. In the time one might spend eating, one could get free food and help the library.

For an event like this focus group, I think the most important way to reach students is by choosing the event time carefully, providing food, and advertising it abundantly throughout campus.

Making Team Rules

Developing ground rules for your team will help ensure that you get off to a good start and keep on that path. "Design team failure is usually due to failed team dynamics,"[4] and establishing rules that the entire team buys into can go a long way in preventing failures in teamwork. In general, ground rules should be developed as a team, but there are some basics that all service design teams should have.

- *Be open.* All ideas are worthy of exploring, because even if you are not going to implement the idea itself, it was generated from a problem.
- *Remember that all members of the team are valuable, and it's important to treat them as such.* This means that one person should not get all the grunt work, while another is doing big thinking and having fun conversations with users. Share tasks equitably and respect one another's time.
- *"Coach more, direct less."*[5] If there are members of your team who are administrators or managers, they should make room for the other team members to stretch and develop their skills. Administrators often have knowledge that impacts the team, and they should be willing to share that or trust will be lost.
- *Don't silo team members.* Everyone on the team will have duties that they are responsible for, but they should still be engaged in other work taking place.
- *Be flexible.* Everything about your project is likely to change in at least some way. Thus, it is essential that the team be flexible about ideas, directions, and one another.

- *Set goals.* Service design is fun, and you can easily enjoy the process so much that you fail to accomplish anything. Make sure you set goals and deadlines to work toward.
- *Accept conflict.* While it is fun, this work is also hard, and everyone will not agree on everything. It is important to accept and work with that conflict or risk team members shutting down.
- *Leave preconceived notions at the door.* We all think we know our users. And maybe some of us do, but let them tell you who they are and what they need.

Defining Scope and Getting Administrative Buy-in

Clearly defining the scope of your project is essential in ensuring its success. The scope drives how much time the project will take, what tools and methods should be used, who will be involved, how much money it will cost, and all other aspects of the project. Ideally, the scope will be defined by the library administration, in conversation with the research team. Because the work is systems-based and you need to hear from the different parts of the library when designing services, the research team's work needs to have approval from the top. It does not matter if your library organization is mostly flat; there are people on staff who will not take the project seriously without administrative approval. Even with that approval, you will have more work to do to get support from other library stakeholders, which we will elaborate on later.

To define scope, ask, "What is the purpose of the project?" There may be a specific question you want to answer. For example, your director may want to find out why reference question statistics are down or what types of spaces students prefer to use in the library or why middle schoolers come to the library but don't take advantage of programming. Or there may be a much bigger project you want to tackle, for instance, developing initial plans for a new library building or library renovation, or you may want to evaluate the library's relationship with an outside organization like a museum to determine what shared collections you can develop and digitize. The scope for service design projects can be massive or relatively small.

One thing to remember when you are defining scope is that service design relies on triangulated evidence for decision-making. This means that you are going to want to attack a problem from more than one angle before you design solutions. Making sure that the scope has clear-cut boundaries will help ensure that the team does not end up getting distracted and chasing after evidence that you don't need for the service you are designing.

Creating an Initial Schedule

Your schedule is likely to change as the project progresses, but starting with a good outline and deadlines for specific tasks can help keep you on track. A good way to think about your schedule is within the context of the service design stages we are laying out here, to include prework, observation, understanding/thinking, and implementation. Everything you do will fit within one or more of the phases. As the process is iterative, everything may not flow in a perfectly straight line, but the tasks should feed into one another so that the prework sets the stage for observation, observation sets the stage for understanding, and so on.

Develop the schedule by working backward, starting with the goals the research team has identified. As with all project-based scheduling, determine when you need to have major deliverables completed and plan accordingly. For example, if you know that you need to decide how to renovate a section of the library by a certain date to request funding, the steps of the service design project need to correspond with that date.

To get started with planning the schedule, print a blank calendar for each month leading up to the deadline and lay them out on a table. Circle the final deadline for completing the entire project or at least one phase. If you do not have a set deadline, ask an administrator for one or make one up. Once you have the beginning and ending dates in front of you, fill out what the research team will do during each week of the project. Be sure to allow plenty of time for the prework (planning) and understanding/thinking (analyzing) phases. While the observation phase often feels like the meat of the service design process, it actually tends to take the least amount of time. Getting ready to observe and then thinking about and collating the observation results requires a significant time commitment.

Getting Support from Library Stakeholders

It is helpful to have administrative buy-in from the very beginning of planning for a service design project. Administration should help define the scope and set boundaries for the project plan; however, their buy-in is only the first step. Getting support from other library staff members is also important because you will need their input and help throughout the process. The key to getting and keeping support is communication. As discussed in chapter 1, libraries are good at making silos. Silos not only lead to staff in one area being unaware of what is going on in another area, but they can also lead to trust issues, especially when there are hierarchical delineations, in addition to functional ones.

Why Use Service Design? A College Librarian's Perspective
By Dena Hutto

At an academically demanding residential liberal arts college like Reed, the success of the library depends on our students feeling that they have ownership of the space. This is a community that deeply loves its traditional library reference room, especially the "thesis tower," also a part of the original 1930 library building. But love isn't everything. Does this building, including four successive additions built between the 1940s and 2000s, provide our students with the kinds of spaces they need to be successful today? The LUX group was charged with discovering how our students experience the library as a whole: the spaces, the service desks, the collections, the website as gateway to substantial electronic resources. The group has been able to provide sound, convincing, broad-based assessments of how students experience the existing library and how they might envision alternative changes, which we are considering. Their work enables me, as a library director, to have confidence in my vision for a library facility that retains a traditional and inspiring sense of intellectual community, while providing the functionality needed by current and future student scholars.

Think carefully about how and what to communicate to library staff about your service design project and process. Most staff members have never heard of service design, but many will be familiar with the idea of usability studies. To simplify your communication, you may want to call on the familiar concepts of usability to draw people in. It is also important to be clear that the team is a recommending body rather than one with decision-making power (if that is true). To fully understand what they are studying, the research team needs to be able to count on hearing honest feedback from the library staff.

You may want to announce the formation of the research team by sending staff an e-mail similar to this one:

> Dear library staff,
>
> I am writing today to announce the creation of the library's service design (SD) team. The SD team will investigate how [insert your user group] thinks about and uses [insert the service you will assess] to decide what reference at [your institution] should look like. As part of its investigation, the SD team will be asking for input from most or all staff members. While the team will not make any decisions about new services in the library, they will provide recommendations on how we can improve the user experience.

Once the team is in place and working, communication should keep going through both formal and informal channels. The team should look for opportunities to talk about their work in staff and departmental meetings, and in casual conversation with users and staff, as a way to keep stakeholders engaged in the process.

Tools

The team lead or the entire research team may want to create an ecology map at the beginning of the project. This tool creates a foundation for the team to refer to throughout the project because it highlights the various interconnections that exist in the library, with the focus of the project at the center and the various interconnections extending outward from there.

Observation Phase

The purpose of the observation phase is to gather data and evidence. In this phase, the research team may start to gather data by conducting initial interviews and possibly sharing a survey with potential participants to get a sense of how often they use and how they see library services. Results may help foster conversation and refine the scope as an initial step in the project. The evidence gathered at this point can be used in discussion groups with the UWG. As discussion moves forward, the research team may veer away from the initial data, but it is still useful in getting the conversation started.

Finding the Anthropologist in the Library

IDEO's Tom Kelley believes that the most important role in innovative design work is the anthropologist, because people who use the discipline and tools of anthropology as their guide are "extremely good at reframing a problem in a new way—informed by their insights from the field—so that the right solution can spark a breakthrough."[6] Observation is key to the power that anthropologists bring to design. Librarians can strive to behave and think like anthropologists by adopting their mindsets and learning to use their tools. If librarians are willing to wear an anthropologist hat when designing services, they are more likely to come up with ideas that truly respond to users' needs and expectations.

Identifying and Understanding Your Users

So who are our users? This is an essential question that must be answered. In addition to having a scope that helps clarify which problems to work on, we need to know who to ask to determine whether the problems the research team has identified are actually problems in the first place. Maybe they are just symptoms of actual problems. Users should also play a role in defining and refining scope.

The ecology map mentioned in the previous stage is a great tool for identifying a core group of users. If you work in a small library at a small liberal arts college, your core user group may be undergraduate students between the ages of 18 and 22. If your library is an urban public library, you may need to do additional research to determine who the users are. What languages are spoken? What age groups use the library most? Are there parents with small children or is this an older community with more retirees? If your library is a special library, your users may be engineers, doctors, lawyers, or other professionals.

Regardless of what type of library you work in, one of your first jobs is to identify the core group(s) of users. After identifying the core group(s), we need to understand how they use library resources. These two objectives, identifying core users and understanding their behavior, are key to the observation phase. After we identify some core user types, we can perform outreach to encourage them to join our newly formed UWG.

Creating a User Working Group

The UWG is the research team's partner and the main group of users that the research team will consult and meet with. They will help the research team understand user behavior and motivation. The research team and the UWG will talk a lot and learn a lot from one another.

The UWG should represent the core user groups as closely as possible. It should be comprised of various members of the communities your library serves. In the case of a small liberal arts college library, the research team may want to recruit two students from each year. For a public library, the UWG may be comprised of adults of different ages, sexes, and occupations. If the library patronage is culturally, ethnically, or linguistically diverse, the research team may opt to ask members from various ethnic or language groups to be part of the UWG. If there is a large teen population, the library may opt to have a teen-only working group. Additional permissions may be required for underage participants.

As with all projects, scheduling may be an issue. Thus, it is best to find times that work for all members of your UWG. We have found that holding discussion groups after normal business hours works best for our students. This is something your research team will need to explore when creating group schedules.

Forming Discussion Groups, Not Focus Groups

During the observation phase, the research team will meet with the UWG and ask them to perform exercises or discuss observations made by the research team. These meetings are discussion groups and not focus groups. Discussion groups are more open than focus groups. They are meetings of the research team and the UWG to discuss a predetermined topic. The purpose is not only to get answers to questions, but also to dig deeper to get at root problems. They are free-flowing conversations, and while the research team may enter the meeting with ideas of questions they have on the topic, the discussion should largely be allowed to follow a course determined by the users. Unlike a focus group, the research team should not create a script with a rigid set of questions for a discussion group. Discussion groups may last for just part of a meeting with the UWG or consume the entire meeting time.

You may leave the discussion group with more questions than when you arrived, but your efforts will lead to greater meaning and understanding as you continue to progress through the service design phases. Focus groups are also a powerful tool, but they are designed to elicit responses based on targeted prompts. In service design, focus groups are often used later in the process, after co-creating proposed solutions with the UWG to test hypotheses and ideas.

Planned exercises are another part of the observation-phase meetings with the UWG. They are based on specific questions designed to elicit a response from each member of the UWG. Using discussion notes and data from documents or artifacts produced as part of the exercise, the research team can discuss the findings with the UWG to reveal deeper meaning and motivations behind the responses. This can be done as part of the meeting, when the exercise has been completed, or at a later meeting, and should lead to deeper insights. Planned exercises can also be a platform for co-creating solutions as you move to the understanding/thinking phase.

Tools

The observation phase is about gathering observational data. While not an exhaustive list, some tools that may help are design ethnography and surveys. While design ethnography is not a single tool, this method is good for capturing a large amount of ethnographic data relatively quickly. Surveys are useful for learning about initial perceptions and reactions to certain things in the environment or verifying a finding. Surveys should never be the only method used to gather observations. Rather, they should be used in conjunction with other methods that require some interaction with users.

If the team is looking at how space is being used or evaluating an area for redesign, a space analysis will be useful. Quantifying the number of patrons in a space at a given time provides a picture of how patrons move through a space and where and when they gather. A space analysis can be used to find space preferences, which provides fodder for a discussion with the UWG. Once enough data has been gathered to create informed composites of users, the research team can create personas. The research team can test hypotheses and solutions using the personality composites. By asking, "How would patron X react in this situation?" of each persona, you can begin to vet solutions. This is a low-impact method for gathering data and insights that can be further analyzed with actual patrons in the next phase.

Understanding/Thinking Phase

The understanding/thinking phase is about synthesizing the data, visualizing behaviors, and creating solutions. While the observation phase is about gathering the initial data, the understanding/thinking phase entails creating insights based on the data and the previous work with the UWG. In this phase, you will use evidence to confirm conclusions by using such additional feedback tools as journals and discussions. The objective is to co-create, refine, and create prototype solutions with the UWG and test them with non-UWG users. Prototypes are rarely perfect the first time, so there may be a period of revisiting the original design, refining it, and then testing it again. We delve deeper into the art of prototyping in chapter 4, but for now the research team should have this on their radar as a thing to do before moving to the next phase.

The UWG is an important part of the entire project, but especially during the understanding/thinking phase. Remember, we don't design for the user, we design with the user.[7] During the observation phase, the UWG guides the research team through their journeys to use the library and its resources. During the understanding/thinking phase, the UWG and the research team create solutions together. Both the research team and the UWG should work together to determine the best solutions with all perspectives in mind. The UWG provides the user perspective, while the research team approaches the task from the library staff perspective. The research team should also come to the project with an agenda to match or exceed user expectations. It is sensible to share that agenda with the UWG from the start, but it should also serve as a reminder to them throughout the process to be honest with their feedback. The necessary elements of the understanding/thinking phase are detailed in the following sections.

Synthesizing, or Data to Insights

Synthesizing data is about identifying patterns in the collected data. Synthesizing involves reading transcripts and notes from the various UWG meetings, analyzing the artifacts produced by the UWG, pulling in other relevant data, and finding connections. Recurring patterns point to potential areas to address further with the UWG and possible areas that could cause users to have a less-than-optimal experience. The goal of synthesis is to turn data into insights to use as the basis for possible solutions. One of the common challenges for research teams when synthesizing data is trying to differentiate whether a finding is reflective of actual behavior or just an anomaly. The UWG can help delineate actual behavior patterns from anomalies.

Visualizing Behavior

Visualizing behavior helps the research team put user behavior in context.[8] The visualization process, via either customer journey mapping or blueprinting, exposes the interconnections throughout the library and highlights potential pinch points in the user journey. In figure 3.1, a member of the library research team is working with a UWG member to help visualize student research behavior. Visualization and mapping exercises are great tools to use when making the case for a change in service delivery. Maps not only provide evidence of current behavior, but can also be used to make the case for a change in how a service should be delivered or where services can be refined for a better user experience.

Co-Creating Solutions

Based on the insights gained by the team thus far, the UWG and the research team can start formulating solutions to problems and pinch points. To do this, the research team and the UWG should hold discussion groups to share ideas. All suggestions and possibilities should be considered until the solutions are analyzed in comparison with the data and the UWG experience. After settling on a possible solution, the team can begin prototyping. The research team should consider discussing possible solutions with frontline staff, as they are another source of expertise in understanding how any changes in service delivery may affect the user experience.

Figure 3.1.   A research-team librarian works with a member of the UWG to help visualize research behavior.

The proposed solutions should not only add value, but also make sense. That means they must do the intended job of solving the problem and work well within the library's aesthetic (and budget). Solutions are not solutions if they aren't fiscally feasible or if the tradeoff to implementing the solution creates additional problems. It is important to be mindful of the bigger picture and what impact, if any, the implemented solution will have on the rest of the library and the overall user experience.

Prototyping and Testing

Prototyping is a "physical representation of an idea."[9] We create prototypes to elicit responses to proposed solutions. Not only do they improve the likelihood that the final implemented solution will work, but they also prevent wasting large sums of money on ideas that end up being mistakes. Using a wardrobe box to represent a service point is cheaper than building a mahogany desk, only to find out that an adjustable desk is the optimal solution. Prototypes need not be elaborate. They simply need to provide a venue for constructive feedback to determine the next steps in solution development. To get appropriate feedback, users need to experience the proposed solutions before they can express what aspects of the new service work or don't work for them.

When the prototype is ready, it is time to test it. This means putting the solution in the physical library (or on the web, if testing a new interface) so users who were not part of the UWG can try it out. If, for example, you are testing a new location for the reference desk, close the current desk and redirect patrons to the prototyped desk. Even if your prototype is a wardrobe box, the patron will eventually get over that fact and ask a question. The material used to construct the prototype does not matter. You can get feedback on the prototype in informal or formal ways by asking questions of users when they use it or by implementing a survey or holding a focus group. The important thing is to provide plenty of opportunities for users to provide feedback. Prototype testing should either confirm that the co-created solution is a good option for implementation or that the team needs to go back to the drawing table.

Refining

If you find that the solution is ineffective, refine and test again. This is why cheap cardboard is a better value for prototyping than mahogany. If a proposed solution doesn't do well in the wild, bring it back to the design space, assemble the UWG, and rework the solution using the feedback given. At some point, the research team and the UWG will get it right. More often than not, you'll get it right by asking users what they want. Co-creating with service design is so powerful because it requires you to understand and work with user needs and expectations.

What Was It Like to Lead a Focus Group? What Advice Would You Give to Other Libraries Attempting to Do the Same Thing?
By Pema McLaughlin

I enjoyed leading focus groups a great deal and was almost never nervous after they got going. But I was always conscious that a balancing act was happening, and that I had to be continually attentive. I think the central problem of leading a focus group is the process of encouraging people to express reactions to the library that they hadn't previously put into words. Focus group participants don't usually think about how they use library space, what their likes or dislikes are, and why they have the instincts they do. The discussions I was facilitating required asking people to be introspective at the same time that they collaborated with the rest of the focus group in formulating their ideas. Because of that, running a focus group was, for me, about worrying whether I would be able to balance provoking people's thoughts, keeping the conversation relaxed, and making sure all the participants could say what they wanted to say. I had to both be ready with my own opinions about using the library to encourage other responses but not overwhelm the early impressions of the other students with things I'd already figured out.

Moving from topic to topic came pretty easily; our plan for issues to cover had a natural flow, and participants often brought related topics up organically. The fact that our plan for questions was based on previous student discussions made it feel very natural to me. But it was easy for the focus group to devolve into me asking a series of questions and participants responding very basically, or at worst with shrugs. Getting beyond that required paying attention to who was enthusiastic and drawing them out, changing the order of questions I asked in response to what the group seemed interested in, and demonstrating my support for whatever participants proposed while refraining from criticism. Perhaps the most important part of the process was getting a sense of what all students in the group's core concerns were: major problems, computer needs, proximity to campus, and familiarity with the space all mattered. First-year students had a very different type of knowledge and reactions than upperclassmen. If student consensus on an issue happened, I wanted it to emerge from difference. It was easy to shallowly push people into agreeing about something but much more valuable to explore the nuances in their experiences and allow them to come to agreements if that felt right to them.

Tools

The understanding/thinking phase is about synthesizing data, creating insights, co-creating solutions, and testing those solutions with actual users. One invaluable tool that can be used as an overlap between observation and understanding/thinking is journaling, performed by members of the UWG. In this exercise, the UWG members each keep a diary of their library interactions or their interactions with similar services for a set amount of time. Journaling helps us reach a deeper level of understanding about specific user behavior.

Scenarios are a tool used to get feedback or ideas from the UWG based on photos of staged library interactions. By prompting the group members to answer questions about the scenarios, you can get a better sense of typical user expectations in a given situation without the need to perform the action in the library. After gathering the data and confirming evidence, the research team may want to create customer journey maps (CJM) based on user journeys to complete a task. CJMs can demonstrate the tightly coupled library environment and help show pinch points or areas of confusion for users. After using these tools and the others detailed in chapter 4, the research team can begin to co-create solutions and prototypes. After testing and refining prototypes, it is time to implement solutions.

Implementation and Post-assessment Phase

The implementation phase is the culmination of your hard work. The research team has done the research, created and learned from the UWG, and tested and refined solutions. It is now ready to go live with a finished solution. We wish there was a tried and true, step-by-step method for implementation, but each library is drastically different. The next steps involve handing over the newly designed service to the new owners or managers of the service.

The research team is not the group responsible for implementing the service. Sometimes the research team will only be responsible for making recommendations, and then the group responsible for the service or the library administration will make the final decision on if and how the service will be implemented. While there may be some members of the team who are members of the group that implements the service, it actually belongs to the functional group that will offer and maintain it.

To ensure that the service is implemented as designed, the research team should blueprint the process and give the documentation to the new owners of the service so they can begin managing it. Documentation provided by the research team to the service owner should include recommendations for management and assessment, including a list of metrics the team can use to evaluate success.

Blueprinting the Service and Selling the Evidence

Blueprinting the service is an essential element of the implementation phase. The blueprint is a document that combines the user journey with the behind-the-scenes actions and resources that are necessary to fulfill a task. These behind-the-scenes or offstage elements demonstrate how integrated the library is. The blueprint can also help with the final orchestration of the service proposition when finally implemented.

After the work has been done and a well-researched and tested solution created, you often have to get final approval, whether from your library director, board, superintendent, provost, or someone else. When this is the case, demonstrate with evidence. Use the evidence you have compiled to create dynamic presentations or reports that sell your findings. Blueprints can be beneficial in these situations because they provide a comprehensive visual of your findings. The important thing is to let the evidence do the talking. Your recommendations should be based on the evidence, so make it clear that you are simply conveying user needs, desires, and expectations.

Measuring Effectiveness

The project does not end with implementation. The research team may be done and has handed the keys to the service over to the managing department, but the work continues. It is wise to consider possible problems that may impact a service during the design process, but it is impossible to anticipate everything. Continual measurement using predefined metrics for success should be an ongoing priority. The ability to measure has never been easier, and there are a number of options to choose from. The research team may be asked to devise a plan for measuring the success of the service.

The most obvious measure of success for any service design project in a library setting is user satisfaction. User satisfaction manifests in repeat usage and potentially an increase in usage by previous nonusers of the service. While user satisfaction may be hard to quantify, the research or management team may want to employ a method for soliciting feedback from users. If a physical touchpoint, placing a box with slips asking, "Tell us what you think about___," or a simple, "How are we doing?" may suffice. If the new service is web-based, you may want to add a link to a feedback form. Whatever method you use, you should try to be unobtrusive and require as little time or effort as possible for the user to find the link or complete the form.

Another measurement method is tracking the number of questions at a touchpoint. For instance, if the team finds that wayfinding is an issue, they might come up with a plan to implement new signs and maps. After the new signs are posted, fewer directional questions should be asked at the service desks. If there is no decrease, there may be a problem with the new signs. Similarly, if there is another process in the library that users always have to ask about and your project is meant to help them find their way through it but the number of questions on how to use it do not decrease, something is not working. Conversely, sometimes the goal is to increase the number of something, whether it be checkouts, appointments, computer or space use, and so on. Monitoring use is a quick and easy way for the manager of the new service to determine if changes are working.

Tools

Blueprints are the most important tool during the implementation phase. They serve two purposes: documenting how a service is performed and confirming the highly integrated nature of the library and its operations.

SUMMARY

Service design happens in phases. While each project will be unique in content, process, and duration, service design projects pass through the following phases:

- Prework: The focus is on project management and planning, creating a research team, assigning roles and tasks, setting ground rules, defining scope, and getting buy-in.
- Observation: The goal is to gather data through observation, surveys, or discussions with the UWG. Initial findings may prompt the research team to refine the scope of the project.
- Understanding/thinking: The focus is on creating solutions by synthesizing, evaluating, and visualizing the data. After creating solutions, the research team can prototype and test with non-UWG users, refining prototypes as needed.
- Implementation and post-assessment: The newly proposed or refined service is released into the wild. While the work of the research team may be complete at this point, the maintenance of the newly proposed solution is handed over to the managing department. At this time, the research team can also share advice and a regimen on how to continue assessing the new service. Post-assessment is key to the long-term success of any project.

Chapter Four

Tools and Techniques

Service design researchers gather data, synthesize it, verify assumptions with a user working group (or actual users), create insights, and co-create solutions with users. Nearly every step of the process involves talking with or working side by side with users to not only inform the team on their behaviors, but also drive the research process. The research team uses tools and techniques in active collaboration with the user working group (UWG) and tries to learn from them throughout the process. After working on exercises aimed at allowing the library researchers to understand them as users, the UWG actually becomes an extension of the research team to facilitate the process of designing *with* them rather than *for* them.[1] After co-creating solutions, the expanded team creates prototypes and tests with additional users to verify the findings. After testing is complete, a final version of the solution is developed, and the research team releases the solution into the wild.

This chapter defines and explains some of the tools and techniques used in service design. Like other chapters in this book, it is not meant to be a step-by-step manual, but rather a description of tools to be used as needed. Use the tool(s) that will best help you answer your research question. Think carefully about the kind of information you want to find out when selecting a tool. For example, if you want to track how many people use a service during a specific period of time, you would use a different tool than you would for finding out why they use that service. If you want to answer both of those questions, you would obviously need to use more than one tool.

THINGS TO CONSIDER

For each tool, we describe and explain why and when you would use it, but the examples are only examples. The research team should experiment and use the tools in whatever way works for it. There is no one way to use any of these tools, and that means there is no wrong or right way. As you collect, analyze, and evaluate your findings, make visualizations to represent your findings and conclusions. The most important aspect of the visualizations used to present service design findings is that findings and recommendations get the point across simply and accurately so that they are not misinterpreted or poorly implemented. Focus on function and evidence first.

Technology

At the time we are writing this book, there are many software options on the market to help with your user experience needs. Use what works best for you and your budget. We recommend focusing less on the software and more on gathering the data. Don't let an interface interfere with your data gathering or influence how the data is gathered. The tools listed here can easily be used with a notepad and a pencil (or a pen, if you prefer). When technology adds value (as in the case of using an audio recorder), take advantage of it. But if you are only counting patrons in a small section, simple hash marks may do the job just as effectively as open-source software. Adapt the tools to fit your environment and resources. There is no one correct method, only your method.

Space and Limitations

Do not allow your work with the data to be limited by space, software, or other logistical details. If you choose to use a spreadsheet to synthesize data, don't let the limitations of the software influence the synthesis. If the best option is to use scraps of paper or, conversely, an entire wall, use what works best. If what you really need is the floor to spread out on, move tables out of the way and use the floor. If a final visualization needs additional content to provide background or additional information, get some tape and add it on. Don't let the technology limit you. Be creative and do what is needed.

Letting Others Influence Your Finished Product

Everyone has an opinion, and some will freely share what they think of your data and your assumptions if they have yet to see the evidence. If you have done the research and gathered the data, you should feel comfortable moving forward with the recommendations and ideas of the research team. At the end of the day, the evidence is in the data. If you are making a final report for an administrator and you need to hire a graphic designer to clean up the finished product, double check their work. Graphic designers will lean toward making a nice layout and fitting the platform. But if the finished visualization needs additional content, make sure it is there. The saying "less is more" is often repeated, but sometimes "more is necessary."

THE TOOLS, WHAT TO EXPECT, AND HOW TO USE THIS CHAPTER

Don Norman has a rule of thumb for spotting bad design: "Look for posted instructions."[2] We couldn't agree more, but we need to break this rule here. The following pages cover seventeen different tools and techniques commonly used in service design projects. This list is not exhaustive, but it should give any team a place to start. These tools have allowed us to unearth what motivates our students to work and use the library as they do.

Each tool description is broken down into six sections: What? Why? How? When? Who? Materials? The purpose of this structure is to break down the bits and pieces of each tool. We hope the nuanced approach allows for comprehension of why a specific tool is useful. For some tools, we include images to help readers visualize how a tool is useful or is performed. Feel free to adapt the tool as you see fit. Service design is still close enough to its infancy that no "correct way" or standard has been created, leaving some wiggle room for creativity and innovation.

THE ECOLOGY MAP

What?

The ecology map serves as a contextual reference to the environment in which a service exists. It is essentially a map of the interconnections in and around a service environment. The map illustrates the various actors that hold a stake in any aspect of the service delivery model. It is particularly helpful at the outset of a project.

Why?

The map displays the tightly coupled nature of the departments, policies, workers, and spaces that feed into the delivered service. By mapping the interconnections, you can better understand the dependencies that exist in a service and allow it to function properly. The map also allows us to see the time, context, actors, and connections required to perform a task or use a service.[3] The mapping process, like a blueprint, shows areas in which you should proceed with caution—especially in potentially political areas—but it can also indicate areas for improvement. Moreover, the mapping process can highlight areas that can be reorganized and potential new service concepts.[4]

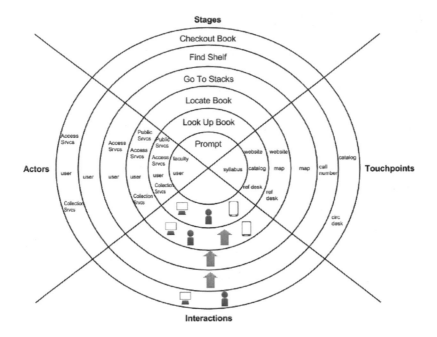

Figure 4.1.   The ecology map.

How?

As with most of the tools in this chapter, there is no one preferred method for creating the map. Start by thinking about what you want to know about the ecology. Four characteristics that should be included are actors (or stakeholders), time (stages), context (touchpoints), and interactions (method of exchange). Determining what is important for your project will influence how the map is displayed and organized.

A good approach is to get the research team together to write down the stakeholders or players, stages, touchpoints, actions, and interactions involved in a service on sticky notes. The stakeholders may be in the library, or they could be external community members. If they are involved or have a stake, write them down. The sticky notes can then be grouped in different ways to display the interconnections, how they are related, and when they relate to one another.

The stage a user is in may determine how different players react to or influence the action. For example, the action of finding a book in the library involves every department, but every department does not influence every stage in the action. When a patron is in the stacks looking for a book, they have already consulted the catalog and have a call number, and now they are focused on finding the physical book. Depending on how a library is organized, this may involve library administration (maps), technical services (spine labels), and circulation (stacks management and reshelving).

Looking at the various stages on the ecology map will also highlight the importance of working with specific departments or stakeholders if a change in action is required. If the team finds that people are struggling with finding a book in the stacks based on poor wayfinding, the members may propose changes to the maps and shelf labels. They may also recommend changing or adding new signage that highlights the contents of a room. In this instance, the ecology map is a tool for the research team to refer to in an effort to ensure that affected departments are made aware of the situation and can help refine the current environment to better meet patron needs.

When?

The ecology map is usually used at the beginning of a project. It serves as a foundational reference tool so the research team can ensure that all stakeholders are consulted and involved with the process and keep track of the various interdependencies that will be affected by any changes.

Who?

While the UWG can help identify stakeholders, this task is best suited for the research team. If the project is being sponsored by another division of the library, it might be best to include them as well.

Materials?

This is a hands-on process. You will need sticky notes and a whiteboard, a big wall, or a table for affixing and rearranging notes. There are software packages that can do similar work, but we prefer a large wall or table with plenty of space to move around so the team can adjust the notes and everyone is able to see them. This allows the research team to take a step back and see the contents, discuss as a group, and reorder as necessary.

SPACE ANALYSIS

What?

Libraries are first and foremost places of learning. Depending on the type of library, they may provide books, public computers, access to the Internet, tables and desks, comfortable seating, meeting or group study spaces, or makerspaces. Measuring how spaces are being used in the library helps ensure that they are well designed and work as they should for users. Space usage analyses go beyond gate count to manually count where users are in the library, when they are using it, and what they are doing there. Space usage is a part of the ethnography group of tools.

Why?

A space analysis in service design should include more than just looking at where users are sitting. When we look at the library as staff members, we see the facilities, furniture, and equipment through a different lens than users. We rarely use the spaces that we provide to patrons so it is imperative that we investigate how they see and use them.[5] Observing how users move furniture around, arrange themselves, and repurpose things provides insight into what may be missing for them. Patrons will adapt their environment in ways to benefit their task and match their preferred working style. Let's look at three examples.

- A single patron is sitting at a large table in the main reading room at 2 p.m. with her laptop open. Next to the laptop she has a tablet computer and her phone, as well as notebooks and books.
- At 11 a.m., two students are working next to one another at a counter space. They have moved a small plastic library sign and are busy typing on their laptops. They are standing next to one another, but it does not appear that they are working together.
- A patron is sitting on the floor reading a book. Her phone is plugged into the wall next to her. The time is about noon.

Our observation data should tell us a few things about these examples. First, the usage data captures the what, where, and when of each patron's library use, providing quantitative data to help understand basic usage patterns. Second, documenting observations about how patrons use the space provides qualitative data that can be used to adapt, refine, or renovate the library. We saw a patron sitting in the main reading room at one of the big, flat tables using multiple computing device, reading materials, and notebooks, indicating that she needed a study area with lots of room to spread out. We also saw students adapting a counter area to turn it into a standing desk and a student sitting on the floor to be close to an electrical outlet. These examples provide considerable content to take to the UWG discussion groups for further exploration.

How?

Counting seems simple, but there are several things to consider when planning for a space usage analysis. How often should you count? Is the counting limited to certain areas of the library? What exactly is going to be counted? What definitions and maps are needed so all staff members count similar behavior accurately? What is in scope and what is out of scope?

Frequency

The research team may decide to count at a specific time every hour for a set number of days. The key in all aspects of counting is consistency.

Geography

Counting specific spaces is important, and defining where a space begins and ends is helpful for all members of the counting team.

Activities and Behavior

What gets counted is also important. The team should decide what types of behaviors or actions should be counted. If there is a pile of books on a table and a bag next to them but no person, does that suggest that a user is sitting there or just passing through that area? Do we count or not? Defining what behaviors should be counted ahead of time will help the team members when they are walking around counting and ensure consistency in the data.

Path

Depending on the actual space to be observed, the research team may want to devise a path through the space that allows for optimal observation as unobtrusively as possible. Coming up with a baseline route for library staff to follow will help with the efficiency and consistency of the count.

Gate Count

The research team may also want to consider capturing the library gate count for the same hour. This may give an overall use of the library to provide a backdrop. If the research team is only counting a specific wing of the library, having a baseline number to compare to will be helpful.

When?

Space usage counting is best done during the early phases of a project and regularly thereafter. The data gathered serves as a foundational reference point as the research team completes individual projects and as they work on projects over the long term. Space analyses can be relatively easy and inexpensive, and part of an ongoing library assessment program.

Who?

Space analysis is best done by the research team. If conducting sweeps over a longer period of time, the team may want to recruit other members of the library staff to assist in counting.

Materials?

Space usage studies can be done with tools as simple as a pencil and notepad. Our research team has used the SUMA software from North Carolina State University.[6] It is open source and can be downloaded and adapted to your library environment.

INTERVIEWS AND CONTEXTUAL INQUIRY

What?

Interviews are an essential part of any service design project. They can be used throughout the process to drive understanding, make connections, and create rapport with users. We use interviewing techniques in most discussions with users, but interviews can also be done as a stand-alone activity.

Why?

The interview process helps build understanding and connection between interviewer and interviewee, and it also can build empathy on the part of the research team.[7] The connection made through conversation is invaluable in understanding who your users really are. Similar to discussion groups in that conversation is the main tool, an interview is a more intimate approach and can help users lower their guard. The user sees the researcher taking the time to get to know them as a person. Where focus groups may not provide enough time for each participant to respond at length, the interview format is designed to gain detailed insights from the user.

How?

The interviewer should do research on the problem being studied and develop an interview protocol, which should include a list of questions and follow-up questions.[8] Feel free to make assumptions based on your research and enter the interview with these assumptions, but still be open to having them challenged. During the interview, you will learn and get clarification from users. It is okay to ask questions you think you know the answers to.[9] Part of the purpose is to build rapport and demonstrate to the user that they are the expert.

Context, as Place

The context, or setting, of the interview can influence the outcome. Make the interviewee feel comfortable. One way to do this is to meet them where they will feel most comfortable. If they have an office or space they would like to meet at, doing so could help them warm up quickly to the conversation, making the interview more fruitful. Going to them also makes it clear that you are willing to make the effort, which can go a long way in building rapport with the interviewee.

Presence

During the interview, the interviewee should have your undivided attention. Look them in the eye and engage them. Be mindful and attentive, removing as many distractions as possible. Don't forget to turn off your ringer.

Open-ended Questions

The interview questions should be open ended. A good place to start is with a list of questions that contain the five Ws and an H (i.e., who, what, where, when, why, and how), and avoid questions that start with "do you" or "would you."[10] These closed-ended questions tend to end abruptly and cause unnecessary awkward silence.

Context, as Time

Context may also play a role in when an interview happens. Contextual inquiries happen in a space that adds relevance to the discussion. For example, if the research team is conducting a space study and members see a patron adapting a flat counter space into a standing desk, they may want to stop the patron and ask them to talk about what they're doing. Contextual inquiries may or may not have the same level of planning as most other types of interviews.

Time also matters in preplanned interviews. For instance, if you know that you want to talk to parents of school-age children about after-school programming, you may want to talk to them about planning for homework help at the beginning of the school year as opposed to close to the winter holidays. They are more likely to be fully engaged with that topic during a time when planning for the school year is dominating their thoughts.

Final Preparations

If you have never or rarely conducted interviews, you may want to practice interviewing other team members or colleagues to prepare, especially if you are nervous. While you want the interview to feel natural, practice helps with flow and managing the conversation. Asking the questions in practice interviews also provides an opportunity to test the questions. Even if you do not need to practice interviewing, you should run through the questions with a small pilot group first. It can be challenging to predict how questions are going to go over with participants. By testing with a pilot group first, you can revise the questions based on the outcomes. If you have a question that did not work or discover that there was something else you wanted to ask, make changes to your interview script. You can still use the results of the pilot group in your findings.

When?

Interviews are done throughout the service design process, starting early in the observation phase. The service design process is marked with various forms of interviewing. The team may want to schedule more formal interviews in the beginning. A combination of formal interviews and contextual inquiry is an especially powerful approach because it allows you to dig deeper with some participants, while getting at issues in the context where they occur with others. This allows the research team to more fully understand both the breadth and depth of issues.

Who?

The research team will write the final interview questions, but they may want to work with stakeholders to determine what to cover during the interview. The participants will include the UWG and other users.

Materials?

Interviews should be held in spaces with minimal distractions. If there are two interviewers, each should have the list of questions and their own writing implement and notepad. If you plan to record the interview, you must clear it with the participant ahead of time and ask them to sign an informed consent form. If you work at a college or university, you may need to get approval to conduct and record the interviews from your Institutional Review Board. Make sure your recording equipment is ready to go (including having backup batteries) prior to the interview so all you have to do is hit record when you start.

SURVEYS

What?

Surveys are a common method for gathering information from a large number of users. They can be quantitative or qualitative, depending on whether they include closed-ended or open-ended questions. Surveys can be distributed electronically or in paper format, and they can be short and simple or long and complex. Because service design is primarily centered on ethnographic methods, survey use tends to be limited to short, pulse-capturing instruments.

Why?

Surveys are used to get a pulse on how and, to some extent, why patrons use a service. They are relatively easy to distribute and can be used to gather information from a large number of users. They are good for getting immediate feedback, but not as good for garnering deeper understandings. Surveys are good "reflections of the organization's climate, but they do not say anything about the deeper values or shared assumptions that are operating."[11]

How?

Surveys are lists of questions that come in many forms. The questions can be multiple choice, short or long answer, binary (e.g., yes or no), scaled (i.e., where the participant rates on a scale of number highest/best to lowest/worst), or multiple answer (i.e., checkboxes that ask the user to select all that apply). They can be helpful when you are trying to get input or feedback from many users.

To avoid contributing to survey fatigue,[12] limit the number of surveys you distribute and be careful with the wording and length.[13] Be clear, simple, and straightforward with your questions and answer choices. Participants are more willing and able to respond in a truthful and timely manner to well-written surveys. To ensure your survey is written correctly, you can create it using questions from previously tested and validated surveys or question banks. If you cannot find established questions that work for your project, the research team can create its own. Writing good questions is not as simple as it sounds. Each question should only ask one thing and have an appropriate answer type. After writing the survey, distribute it to the UWG, colleagues, library staff members, or anyone else willing to provide feedback on the structure of the questions and the general design of the survey.

When?

When to distribute a survey depends on your goal for conducting it. The research team will want to think about how many surveys they expect to administer during a given period. You may want to administer a survey to take a pulse, to get information about a specific event, or in situ.

Taking a Pulse

A survey can be given at any time if the research team is looking to take the pulse of patrons. For example, you may want to send a survey to the UWG before an initial meeting to get a sense of what the members know about the library. This information can be used to help sculpt the initial structure and discussions of the meetings with the UWG.

Getting Information about a Specific Event

If you are looking for feedback on a specific event, conducting the survey before, during, or directly after may be appropriate.

Surveying in Situ

Sometimes the research team wants to focus the user's attention on a single service. Placing short surveys near where a service takes place emphasizes the context. For in situ surveys, it is best to make them short and to the point. If the amount of time to complete a survey outweighs the usefulness in the user's mind, they will not respond.

Who?

Surveys are usually created by the research team. In certain situations, the research team may want to work with the UWG to co-create surveys based on discussions about services or resources.

Materials?

Online forms are popular and (too) easy to create and distribute. They come in different flavors and can be distributed via e-mail or social media. The form a survey takes will depend on who you want to question. If taking the pulse of a large patronage, you may want to send the survey via e-mail. E-mail may also work for a small group, but it will depend on the type of questions. For most in situ surveys, you will need paper, pencils, and a collection box of sorts.

PERSONAS

What?

Personas are composites of actual library users. The data used to create the composites comes from the research on users and their behavior. The document text for each persona (see figure 4.2), is a story about a fictional user that conveys important traits, behaviors, and preferences.[14] Personas can be used during the design phase to help build solutions for specific user types.

Why?

Personas help define key elements and behavioral traits found in a group of users. These behavioral types and ways of thinking are represented by a fictional personality created by the research team. These can then be used to help the research team think through how different users might respond to solutions. Personas can also help define who your stakeholders and users are.

How?

You will get to know your users well during the observation and early understanding/thinking phases. After watching, interviewing, and listening to them, and reflecting as a team on the data gathered, you will find patterns in user behavior and motivation. Capture those general traits and create the composites of personalities and behaviors you believe represent your user base. You should limit the personas created to a manageable number, but they should also represent your users broadly. Let's take a closer look at an example of a persona.

Figure 4.2 shows an example of a persona. It includes a name, picture, and narrative about the fictional user. The narrative is about the person's "attitudes, goals, and behaviors"[15] to help the research team focus on actual users when designing solutions. Create as few personas as possible but "as many personas as it takes to express the unique behavior patterns and goals you observed."[16] The names and faces used for the personas should be fictionalized. Don't name the persona after an actual user that the team thinks has traits similar to the composite. By doing so, the team risks confusing the persona with the real person, which can move the focus away from the behaviors and toward the person.

When?

Personas can be created early in the overall process, during the observation phase, although the team may want to delay doing so until the early stages of

Madeline

Undergraduate
Anthropology and Mathematics, double major
19 years old

*I just love working in the library! It is my
favorite place on campus to study because I
can always find a quiet space.*

Madeline is an outgoing, independent student and a dedicated library user. She loves studying in
the library. She currently lives off-campus and has to access resources via the proxy. She likes to
find the answers herself, but loves the chat service on the library homepage. She starts her
searches in Google Scholar before moving over to the subscription databases for more power
searching. She has two spots in the library, one for reading and one for writing.

Library Use
- Uses library as a place to read and write
- Primarily does most of her research from off-campus
- Heavy Google Scholar user for initial article research before switching to subscription
  databases for more serious work

Technology
- Laptop user
- Prefers to read and annotate articles electronically
- Doesn't use library computers unless needed for software

Study Preferences
- Studies (reading) in Science Periodical Room "to be seen" (primary spot)
- Prefers to write in SE Stacks (Flr 2) (secondary spot)

Pain Points
- Wishes the library had more signage
- Thinks first year students need to be more quiet in the library
- Citation management

Figure 4.2.   Persona of the undergraduate student.

understanding/thinking to ensure that enough information about library users
has been collected.

Who?

The research team should ask users and UWG members a lot of questions
during interviews to better understand the attitudes, behaviors, and motivations of the typical library user.

Materials?

The process by which personas are made is interview intensive. The research
team should use the data it has gathered and a whiteboard or sticky notes to
organize traits to create personas. Stock images or drawings can be used for
the pictures.

SERVICE SAFARI

What?

A service safari looks at services "in the wild" with the user. It can be a literal or figurative walk to observe services or a discussion of service experiences. The research team might ask users about their experiences at a coffee shop, shopping at a local grocery store, filling up their cars with gas, buying plane tickets, or going to a movie theater. The services need not be representative of or similar to library services. The goal is to spark a conversation about good versus bad services.

Why?

We examine services to get a better understanding of what users think of when they think of a service and what they consider good and bad service. This gives the research team an introduction into how the user thinks. The service safari can also be used to educate users about services. Services are intangible, but when we start talking about them and put the user in a position to "see" them, they can do a better job of evaluating them.

How?

Depending on your research environment, researchers and users can walk to view, experience, and talk about services. We highly encourage looking at services outside the library. You want to get a reaction to commonly used services, but not the services you'll be studying as part of your research. Focus your questions on emotions and how the user feels about the service. For example, the research team could ask the UWG where they go to get their daily caffeine fix. The UWG may share that they prefer to go to smaller local coffee shops rather than larger chain shops because they like the personal touch. But that opinion might change when asked about shopping for fruits and vegetables, in which case members may opt for a larger grocer with a wider selection of organic produce available throughout the year. This positions the research team to get at the emotional ties and motivation behind user decision-making. Why is one service better than the other? Is the coffee at the smaller local coffee shop better? Is it cheaper?

When?

Service safaris are used to get researchers and participants thinking and talking about services. This is best done in the early stages of any research study and serves as a great ice breaker to any discussion or focus group.

Who?

The research team should lead this discussion. This is a discussion-based technique that is best suited to an open environment.

Materials?

A notepad and pencil will suffice in most instances, but you could opt to use an audio or video recorder. The majority of what happens during a service safari is walking and talking about services the user uses and why.

DISCUSSION GROUP

What?

Much of what happens between the research team and the UWG involves discussing various ideas about library usability. Discussion sessions are typically simple in structure. The research team develops a short outline of topics or questions it wants to address. The purpose of the outline is to help get the conversation started, but it should not be overly prescriptive or lead participants to specific answers. Rather than enter into a discussion group with ideas that you want to hear, the discussion should flow organically. Discussions require a give-and-take between the UWG and the research team. The research team should create a rough structure for the discussion and have certain goals in mind, but the users should lead the actual discussion, with nudging from the research team to elaborate on certain points. Discussion groups are often more about the trip than the original destination.

Why?

Whereas focus groups are geared toward reacting to ideas, discussion groups are focused on synthesizing ideas into insights and eventual solutions. The discussion involves conversation about a topic, with the goal of getting at the meaning behind the things users do and why they do them.

How?

Discussion groups only have light agendas. The agenda is in the form of a few bullet points to cover. A modest list of topics allows the discussion to flow more naturally. The order of topics depends on the amount of time a research team has with the UWG and should start with the most pressing questions, allowing space for verbal meandering.

Depending on the size of the research and UWG teams, the dynamics of the discussion could be influenced by seating arrangement. We highly recommend having the participants intermingle. The research team might want to arrive early to position themselves so that the UWG is not seated on one side of the table or room and the research team on the other. The intermingling of people and teams creates a conversational atmosphere in which participants face one another, with no head of the table. Discussion groups can happen anywhere that everyone can hear one another. Picking a setting that makes the UWG feel comfortable may also be something to consider. Props are not necessary, but the research team may want to bring visuals that can help spark conversation or get everyone on the same page about a space, service, or idea. For instance, when discussing a specific space, the research team may want to bring in maps or pictures.

In chapter 3, we discussed the role of the notetaker. Notetaking is essential during discussion sessions. The research team may opt to have an audio recorder present. Having at least two people take notes at the same time is important because they can note observations about how people look and act, and other nonverbal behaviors. Similar to experiences, no two people will see, hear, or put emphasis on the same thing. All members of the research team should be engaged and ready to reflect on the session later, but only the notetakers should write. Everyone else should be involved in the discussion. We recommend against the discussion lead taking notes because it is his or her job to engage with the UWG, foster the conversation, and move the discussion along if it begins to slow or lag.

The entire discussion session does not have to happen out loud. If you pose a question to the UWG, the verbal response can trigger additional conversation, and participants may adjust their responses based on what others have said.[17] Sometimes the response the research team wants comes from individual members rather than the entire group. Using index cards to solicit responses to inquiries prior to getting a verbal response from the entire group can help provide additional details and insight into how many users feel. You can also see if people seem to change their minds about a topic during the course of the discussion because they either learned more about it or did not have a strong opinion to begin with.

When?

Discussion groups just happen. They are less of a tool and more of a platform for getting at deeper levels of insight. We should say that any time members of the research team get together with the UWG, they are having a discussion group. The main difference is that they are scheduled versus contextual inquiries, which are more impromptu and context-specific.

Who?

The research team creates the outline or agenda. But unlike organizational meetings that have long, bulleted agendas, the discussion group will have a few topics to cover, with the focus on the UWG leading the way and the research team being along for the ride. Remember that this is less about the destination and more about the journey.

Materials?

The research team may opt for a very basic approach. A list of questions and some comfortable seating might suffice. An audio recorder is nice to have, but notetakers are essential.

DESIGN ETHNOGRAPHY

What?

Design ethnography is the use of primarily qualitative research methods to capture insights into user behavior. It is not a single tool or activity, but rather a combination of tools and techniques, including contextual inquiry, interviews, observation, and photography. The goal is to bring to the surface "broad patterns of everyday life that are important and relevant specifically for the conception, design, and development of new products and services."[18] Traditional ethnography is the documentation of how and why people do things within a given context. Design ethnography uses traditional ethnography tools on an accelerated scale. It was born out of a need to "better understand complex work and learning situations in corporate- and public-sector production and service organizations."[19] Our goal is to capture behavior in all its nuances in the context of a library setting.

While design ethnography is mostly qualitative, quantitative methods can be used to complement the qualitative findings either at the start of a project, when the team is beginning to explore and contextualize the problem, or later, to reinforce a finding. A service design project may not have a quantitative component, but it must always include qualitative methods because we are looking for why users behave the way they do. Interviews, focus groups, and discussions are also important in understanding the full picture of why people in a specific situation behave the way they do. Design ethnography is a means to understand nuance and compile the ethnographic record via "vulgar competence,"[20] which are "ordinary competences that are in common use in the setting."[21] Thus, it is a "requirement that the fieldworker become thoroughly acquainted with them."[22]

Why?

Geertz credits Max Weber with saying, "'[M]an is an animal suspended in webs of significance he himself has spun.' I take culture to be those webs, and the analysis of it to be therefore not an experimental science in search of law but an interpretive one in search of meaning."[23] Design ethnography can help you understand the webs of significance that your patrons spin inside the library environment to get at the core motivation behind behavior.[24] We want to know why and how people use the library so we can build a detailed understanding of our users. Once we know this, we are better prepared to meet or exceed user expectations.

How?

Unlike traditional academic ethnography, design ethnography is limited by time, access to users, and workplace demands.[25] Due to time constraints and limited staffing typical of libraries, there is often a sense of urgency when conducting ethnographic studies. Workplace limitations force us to configure ethnography to fit within our workplace lives and the lives and schedules of study participants. It is imperative to gain as many relevant insights as possible within the given time frame. To ensure that the insights gathered are relevant, the team should have a clearly designed scope and use methods that fit the research question and are feasible for the team and participants to accomplish.

As a collection of activities combined to create a fuller picture of user behavior, ethnography can be done through interviews, observations, focus groups, participant journals, contextual inquiry, photography, diagrams, and maps.[26] The UWG will be a major source of information. Using the discussion-group meetings as the platform, the research team and the UWG will complete exercises designed to prompt the group to talk about and dissect their library experiences and behaviors.

The research team should hold planning discussions during the prework phase to develop a focus for their ethnographic work and a preliminary plan of tools and techniques. After devising the focus for the project, the tools should reveal themselves. For example, the first step may be to look at how patrons use a certain wing of the library to find out if additional seating or tables are required due to a recent influx of residents to the area. The team may decide to do a quantitative space usage study, along with observing how the space is being used. After gathering initial data, the team can move to contextual inquiries, talking to patrons throughout the course of a day about why they chose that space. After gathering several layers of data about how and why the space is being used, the team may decide they are ready to co-create solutions with the UWG and other user volunteers. These steps are part of a larger process of ethnography and each step is informed by the previous step.

At the end of this process, the research team will not only have a better sense of who their patrons are, but they will also have developed a deeper understanding of how patrons use the library, what their needs and expectations are, and how best to meet or exceed those expectations. The team will have gone from vulgar competence to thick description. They will know the stories of their patrons and be in a good position to help form worthwhile library experiences.

When?

The research team continuously adds to the layers of ethnography as they move through the phases of service design. Ethnographic methods may be used during any phase of the project, but they are a primary component of the observation and understanding/thinking phases. The research team generally gathers data during the observation phase, to create a composite of users, user needs, and user behaviors so it can enter the understanding/thinking phase with enough insight to propose solutions to the UWG.

Who?

The research team should conduct the ethnographic research. The UWG or other users may help inform the research team, but the study itself should be managed and directed by the research team. This is one part of the service design process where it takes an outside-looking-in perspective. The research team must be mindful of their biases and how they might influence a finding.

Materials?

Ethnography can be done with many different tools, including notepads and pens, video and audio recorders, cameras, and clickers for counting.

CUSTOMER JOURNEY MAPPING

What?

The customer journey map (CJM) is a visual representation of the steps a user takes to perform a task or use a service.[27] By mapping the user's journey, you can more clearly understand the entire process users must go through to accomplish something. It allows you to visualize the interconnectedness of the service ecology and can be used to emphasize the roles different departments play as users journey through library services. The CJM places the user in the center and shows the steps he or she takes and how much time is spent interacting with prompts and touchpoints. The CJM can be used to retrace a physical journey or outline a process, such as how a patron conducts research.

Why?

No other tool in service design provides a better view of the library ecology from the user's perspective than the CJM. As is the case with most aspects of service design, the process of making the map is equally important.[28] When properly executed, the CJM "involve[s] all the different parts of an organization"[29] and helps take library staff "out of the weeds and see the customer experience beyond their silo."[30]

The map helps reinforce the idea that performing tasks in libraries have varying degrees of complexity.[31] By visualizing this complexity, we can identify parts of the process that may create problems for users or find extra steps that can be eliminated to better streamline the process.

How?

To create a CJM, the research team should work closely with the user to trace his or her steps in performing a task. The team can have the user recreate the journey using a whiteboard or sticky notes. Regardless of the materials or method used, the research team will want to dig deeper every step of the way and hear the verbal journey from the user to build an understanding of why specific steps are taken. The discussion should highlight emotions tied to the journey. Note emotional states and any feelings of anxiety with numbers or colors on the map to signify user feelings while completing the task. There is no one set template for how a final CJM should look. The following example (see figure 4.3) has three input areas: prompts or touchpoints (section 1), stages (section 2), and the actual path taken (section 3).

User input is essential when piecing together the various steps of the user journey. The example in figure 4.4 is a CJM that visualizes the user's journey to retrieve a book from the stacks. The circles represent a prompt or the user interacting with a touchpoint. The lines connecting the circles show the path taken. Time is represented in the horizontal area above the path portion of the map.

While it represents a normal task repeated multiple times each day, the CJM highlights the moving pieces in the puzzle to demonstrate the tightly coupled nature of the library and where the potential for failure exists. By working closely with users to create the map and further analyzing the map as a research team, you can locate points of confusion or lack of clarity in what to do or where to go next in the process (see figure 4.5). Potential

Figure 4.3. Customer journey map divided by region.

problems or pinch points are represented by the cloud icon, and decisions are represented by diamonds.

The research team may want to investigate and dig deeper to understand what is causing problems where there is a cloud. Does the user interface in the catalog make sense? Is it clear where the call number is? And do they know they have to write the call number down? If writing is required, is there enough paper at the kiosk and a pencil or pen? When they go to the map, is the map oriented the right way based on its location in the library, and is it clear where the user is in the library? And when they finally get to the correct part of the library, can they find the correct shelf where the book resides? Are the call numbers prominently displayed at the end of the shelves? And finally, are the books reshelved in the proper order?

As we begin to see the complexity involved in performing a routine task, we see the depths of interconnectedness and synchronization required to provide an optimal user experience. At any stage in the process, the user can potentially trip up and have a bad experience. These obstacles can involve anything from the lack of a pencil at a kiosk to a book being improperly reshelved. While some might argue that the lack of a pencil at a kiosk does not hold the same weight as a book being improperly reshelved, the CJM shows how each piece of the journey's puzzle can make or break the user experience.

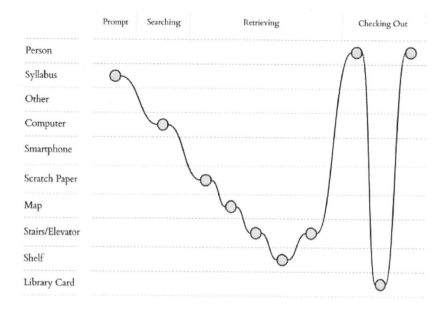

Figure 4.4. Customer journey map detailing the user's journey to check out a book.

Emotional state may not figure into every final product, but it is something the research team may want to document in their notes. Poor lighting or a feeling of discomfort, while specific to any individual user, may also highlight something in the environment that may be addressed with minimal effort, for example, better lighting, improved signage, or adjusting the temperature. As mentioned earlier, the CJM can also highlight a process, such as the steps a user takes to conduct research. To document a process, the map should be adapted to show the thought process, as well as the prompts or external inputs, incorporating an additional layer of concepts in the final map.

When?

The CJM is best done during the understanding/thinking phase. At this point in the project, the research team will have worked closely with the UWG and will be in a position to explore more deeply some of the specifics about the user experience.

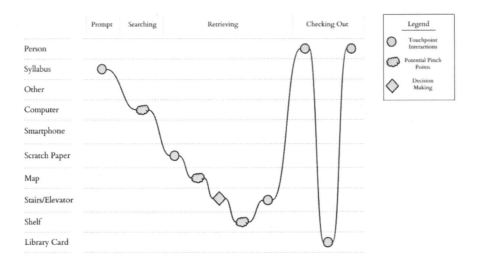

Figure 4.5.   Customer journey map highlighting pinch and decision points.

Who?

The CJM is a co-creation between the research team and the UWG. The research team should lead the discussion but allow the user to take them on their journey, asking a lot of open-ended questions to clarify the physical and mental stages the user passes through.

Materials?

A CJM can be created with markers and pens. Different ink colors can be used to highlight difficulties or pleasing moments or to categorize various aspects of their journey. This is a highly interactive exercise and may involve walking through the physical library. Provide the user with access to every touchpoint so they can completely recreate their journey.

JOURNALING

What?

A journal or diary is a chronological record of a person's activities and thoughts. It may focus on a single event or the repeat interaction a participant has with a service or space. While written journals are the most common format, alternate options, for example, photo and video diaries, can also be informative. Regardless of format, the most important function of the journal is serving a record of thoughts and feelings about activities performed.

Why?

Journaling allows the research team to be a fly on the wall and "learn more insights that might not be shared in a traditional focus-group setting."[32] This method "affords at least the possibility of gaining some degree of access to naturally occurring sequences of activity, as well as raising pertinent questions about their meaning and significance."[33] The emphasis of the diary's contents is on the user, not only as the creator of the content and a user, but also as observer.[34] The diary provides an "observational log maintained by subjects which can then be used as a basis for intensive interviewing"[35] Journaling also offers the research team data on how the user interacts with a service, the role they play in co-producing it,[36] and how they feel about it. This tool is a personal and intimate look into user "decisions, preferences, and attitudes."[37]

How?

The research team should create a prompt for users to guide their journaling process. The prompt should be sufficiently broad enough that users have enough to write about. For example, you may be interested in how users interact with a specific service or the library, or how they work on a research project for a set amount of time. In our own research at Reed College, and as seen in figure 4.6, we asked the members of our UWG to document their interactions with the library during the course of a week. This includes not just physically studying in the library, but also accessing databases and other electronic resources from off-campus. The diary was an eye-opening look at how they used the library and their study habits.

The journal can take many forms. The most common is a written diary format, but alternate methods are acceptable. The user may opt to document his or her experience by video or audio, or with pictures. The research team may want to let the user decide which method works best for them because they may come up with a unique way to document their experiences that provides additional insight into the user and their behavior. Set deadlines for diary submissions. Deadlines are a powerful motivator, so while you should work with the UWG members' schedules, be sure to set a deadline so they will actually turn them in.

After gathering the diary submissions, the research team's job is to mine them for insights. Follow up with discussions with UWG members, either one-on-one or in a group setting, to better understand the behaviors and thoughts described in the journal entries. A close reading of the diaries can be

Library Use Diary

Friday, April 18th:
- SWG meeting, 3-4:30
- Working in old pit (hate the name, love the place) from 4:30pm – 6pm
- Notes:
    o It would be great if the outlet under the Northern main desk in the old pit was fixed; one of them is jammed, which is inconvenient when there are many people at this table
    o Some of the chairs here do not have felt bits under their legs so they do not slide properly

Saturday, April 19th:
- Working in my usual spot, 11:30am – 6:00pm
- Using Jstor, Zotero to work on research project
- Went to the Research Methods sociology course page to find other databases besides jstor, since I recently learned about jstor's 5-year lag/moving wall and this project is based around a phenomenon of particularly recent salience
    o Used academic search premier – I wish I could search within only sociological journals, as in jstor!
- Sent an email to the ILL people to resubmit a request for an article – they canceled it because Reed has online access to the article, but the article was badly scanned and is unreadable.

Sunday, April 20th:
- In my normal spot, 10:45am – 6:00pm
- Using Jstor, Academic Search Premier, and Zotero again for the same project as yesterday
- Requested two books through Summit
- Found a book online that I have noticed by chance in the library stacks (I remember because I always think its title is clever—*Trick or Treatment: The Undeniable Facts about Alternative Medicine*)! Went to retrieve it, and found two others nearby that look promising for my project
- Found a book online that I want to read. Searched for it on the library website, but couldn't find it (tried shortening the title, tried by author, etc.). Thought it

Figure 4.6. User journal entry.

used to formulate questions to ask the user to clarify emotions or behaviors noted in the diary. Let's take a look at this process using our Reed example.

Figure 4.6 is a student's diary of her library use during a span of three days. This example has extensive detail about how and where she studies and her feelings and thoughts on various library spaces and services. There are moments of epiphany, as well as more reflexive moments, as she realizes her own ways of working within the library environment. Figure 4.7 shows our team's preliminary analysis of the diary.

The research team's analyses appear in callouts to the right of the diary text. The diary not only shows us how the student works in the library, but also key bits and pieces that contributed to her overall experience. We were

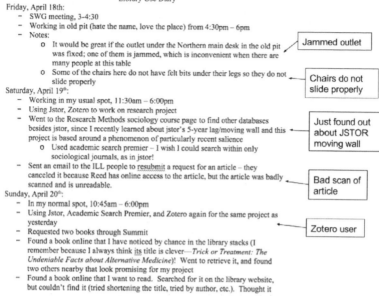

Figure 4.7. User journal entry with synthesis comments.

able to locate the pinch points, or service failures, in her experience. She documented jammed outlets, chairs that got stuck under tables, and poorly scanned articles from ILL. The research team can take this information to the relevant staff and investigate why these failures happened and look for solutions to improve the experience. We may also find that they are symptomatic of bigger underlying issues.[38]

While not related to traditional ideas of the user experience, we also learned that the student just found out about JSTOR's moving wall and that she uses Zotero for citation management. Both are good to know about. Now that we've identified her as a Zotero user, we can ask her more questions about how she discovered it, why she uses it, if she has friends or classmates who use it, or other questions. We could ask the same things and more about JSTOR, but based on her comment alone, we know there is at least one dedicated library user who we would consider advanced who did not know about the moving wall. How many other students is that true of? After asking more questions and digging a bit deeper, we may find that we need to do a better job of teaching students about JSTOR's limitations in our instruction sessions or providing better descriptions on the library website.

When?

The journaling exercise is best done during the understanding/thinking phase. It can be especially useful at the beginning of the process because it can help the research team get better acquainted with the members of the UWG and build rapport between the two groups. It is also a reflective exercise that allows users to provide insights into their own behavior. These captured moments can be beneficial as the team begins exploring issues and problems that need to be addressed.

Who?

The research team provides guidance and scope for the diaries in the form of a prompt provided to the UWG. The UWG members create the diaries, and the UWG and the research team meet to discuss them.

Materials?

Users may opt to use paper and pen or pencil, video, photos, or audio recordings to enhance or give depth to their entries. Our suggestion is let the users work with their preferred medium, as long as the medium or format does not detract from the content. The research team may suggest a preferred format if they don't have the ability to collect or process certain types of digital media.

SCENARIOS AND EXPECTATION MAPPING

What?

Scenarios and expectation mapping is an exercise that allows the research team to place a patron in a real-life library situation for the purpose of providing information on how they feel about and what they expect in various situations. Scenarios and expectation mapping are best applied to specific situations. The research team may opt to use photos to present the scenario or take users to a predetermined location to view the scenario in action.

Why?

Perform the scenarios exercise to hear what patrons expect in certain situations. This exercise provides an opportunity to better understand a patron's emotional and intellectual response to a situation. By using a visual prompt, the research team can conduct the exercise in a discussion setting.

How?

The research team should first determine specific situations on which to focus their efforts. Then decide how to present the scenario—it can either be staged or live. A staged scenario allows the research team to control the environment and remove any noise or other distractions. Running a scenario in a live setting allows participants to more fully experience the scenario, but it may alter the dynamic and cause the UWG to lose focus if there are distractions or if it takes place in a quiet area that is not conducive to talking.

Things to consider when creating a scenario are the staging of the image, the prompt for the UWG to respond to, and how the team wants to receive feedback. Let's look at an example and address each aspect. For example, in figure 4.8, a student is holding a piece of paper, looking at a wall map. A librarian is looking at the reference desk computer in the background. There are no other people or distractions in the picture. Thus, participants can focus on only the relevant aspects of the scenario. By carefully staging the photo, any unnecessary elements can be eliminated so participants can focus and respond to the prompt.

The research team staged the scenario in this picture to emphasize proximity. The key component in this situation is the distance from the wall map to the reference desk where a librarian usually sits. The camera angle is intentional to capture as much of the immediate environment as possible. Our focus is on where the student is in relation to the closest touchpoint in case they need help. The users who responded to this scenario know the library and how quiet this section is, so the image alone provides enough information to help the UWG remember the situation.

To eliminate as much bias as possible, the prompt is written for the UWG to read and interpret. Showing scenarios and prompts to the library staff ahead of time can help you get the wording correct. It is important to test the test to ensure that it directly addresses the right question. Finally, consider how you want to receive feedback. It is likely that the scenarios will be presented in a group discussion. The research team may want to ask participants to initially respond to the prompt on index cards to allow them to answer without outside influence. The research team can then opt to hold a larger general discussion after collecting the cards.

When?

Scenarios work best as part of the understanding/thinking phase. They may be most effective after developing some rapport with the UWG or participants. They can also help build rapport because they are a good way to focus group discussions at the start of a project.

A student is looking to find a book. She has a call number on a slip of paper and is looking at the map by the Reference Desk. A librarian sits at the desk.

Figure 4.8.   A scenario depicts a scene from the library.

Who?

The research team will create the scenarios to present to the UWG or other participants.

Materials?

You will need a camera (or phone) to take photos, simple presentation software to mash up the image and text prompts, and possibly index cards for collecting responses.

WHAT IF . . .

What?

"What if . . ." is a prompting technique used to introduce new ideas in a discussion session or focus group.

Why?

The "what if" technique introduces new ideas for obtaining feedback. The research team may want to introduce new material, ideas, or topics that participants have not brought up or that they want feedback on without unintentionally swaying opinions. Using "what if" can help because the approach is open and invites honest opinion. It helps participants feel like they are working *with* the research team to solve a problem. For example, a research team working with a UWG in a public library may want to get feedback and ideas on how to use a section of the library. During a meeting with the UWG, they may talk about the seating or what type of tables would be best in that space. This could be a great opportunity for the research team to say, "What if we put up walls and make that space into a meeting room?" By introducing the idea in this way, the team is not trying to sway the opinion of the UWG, but is simply offering something new that participants may not have previously considered. The light touch of the "what if" approach allows people to feel comfortable responding to or digging deeper into ideas.

How?

Introducing a "what if" is as simple as asking a question. At the conclusion of a participant thought, the discussion lead may want to say, "Well, what if . . ." The participant will not think twice about this new information being introduced and will respond as if it is part of the normal conversation being conducted in the discussion session.

When?

The best time for a "what if" is when talking with the UWG, when speaking with a participant in an interview, or as a follow-up question in a focus group. It is useful any time a new piece of information would help move the conversation forward.

Who?

The discussion lead will most likely introduce "what ifs," but other team members may also bring them up as follow-up questions in discussion meetings or focus groups. The research team may want to discuss if and when "what ifs" should be included and who should ask the question.

Materials?

This technique can be used in discussion, focus group, or interview settings, and no additional materials are required.

"FIVE WHYS"

What?

The "five whys" is a method for root cause analysis. First pioneered by Toyota in the 1950s, this is a widely used, simple method for better understanding why things happen the way they do. It involves asking users or stakeholders why five times to understand the root cause of a problem.

Why?

Asking why five times allows you to "explore a specific problem in greater depth."[39] The research team should not see problems as negatives, but as a "*kaizen* (continuous improvement) opportunity in disguise."[40] Problems provide opportunities to fix something that is not working, and the "five whys" provide the team with a way to get to the root of what is causing a problem. The "five whys" technique also allows the team to differentiate between actual problems and symptoms. They are not the same, nor should they be treated equally. Understanding the difference between problems and symptoms can help the research team decide where to focus their questions and how to address symptoms.

How?

The "five whys" technique is a fairly simple method. Start by asking a "why" question about the problem and then ask "why" in response to the answers given. For example, let's find out why a patron never received a book requested from a consortial lending partner.

1. Why didn't the patron get her book? Because the consortial lending libraries never received the request.
2. Why didn't the other libraries receive the request? Because our catalog never received (and thus never sent) the request.
3. Why didn't our catalog receive or send the request? Because the requesting link in our catalog is broken.
4. Why is the requesting link in the catalog broken? Because the code update that was sent via e-mail from the vendor was never updated by the web services librarian.

5. Why didn't the web services librarian update the code that was sent via e-mail? Because his inbox is swamped with other consortial e-mails, and he never saw the update e-mail.

As we dig deeper, we are able see that links need to be maintained for a patron to submit a request. If the link is broken or not updated, the request won't work. But we have also learned something about how the web services librarian operates. There may be an underlying problem that this is just a symptom of. He said he is getting too many e-mails and missed a crucial update from the vendor, which could indicate communication issues. If the librarians in charge of maintaining the front end of the system are getting so many vendor e-mails of low importance that they have stopped paying attention to most of them, it may be advantageous to create an alternate method for releasing important updates.

When?

Use the "five whys" when you are trying to find a root cause. This method can be used at any phase of the service design process. The research team can use the "five whys" in discussion sessions with the UWG or other stakeholders to identify the root cause of a problem and get at deeper levels of motivation behind a root cause.

Who?

The research team can use the "five whys" when discussing issues with the UWG or interviewing other stakeholders.

Materials

This technique is a verbal exchange. No additional materials are needed.

PROTOTYPING

What?

Prototypes are physical or experiential representations of ideas. When designing new services, prototypes provide users with a representation of a new service that they can interact with and provide feedback about. The prototype feedback is used to refine the service prior to investing in implementation.

Why?

Prototypes function to "increase the flow of new ideas."[41] They are representations that fill the gap between an idea on paper and what a new service will be like. The prototyping process causes the "willing suspension of disbelief"[42] by giving users a model of how the service will look and feel.

How?

"Prototypes should command only as much time, effort, and investment as are needed to generate useful feedback and evolve an idea."[43] Prototypes can be very rough or highly refined. Their job is to help bridge the gap in the mind of the user so the user can visualize the new service. Because prototypes are used to generate feedback, they can come in any form. For example, if your team is trying to decide where to relocate a service desk, you can use a large box to simulate the new placement of the desk (see figures 4.9 and 4.10). We used this example to explore possible reference desk locations during a space usage project at Reed College. The initial reaction from the UWG was to laugh, because rarely do you see a librarian hauling a beaten up wardrobe box through the library. But when the box was laid on its side, the UWG was able to visualize the reference desk in a new location. After laying the box on two dollies, the research team and the UWG rolled the new "desk" to different spots. The UWG had fun with this exercise and provided valuable opinions on how the flow, noise, and aesthetics of the library could be impacted by the different locations.

Building on the use of a cardboard box to simulate a new reference desk, we can also use what we refer to as a low-tech hologram to show what a new service or touchpoint will look like (see figures 4.11 and 4.12). A transparency sheet showing the outline of the new touchpoint can simulate the appearance of a touchpoint in context. You can also create a mock-up using a photograph and a drawing application to sketch the outline of the service point. The advantage of the former method is that it requires the user to be in the context of the actual possible service. The latter method is best when used for sharing or in a presentation. The low-tech hologram has minimal impact, can be done cheaply and quickly, and only asks the user to bridge the gap between reality (i.e., what they currently see as an empty space) and possibility (i.e., what we propose to do with that space). We also think it has a cool name.

Figure 4.9.   Wardrobe box before prototyping.

Figure 4.10.   Wardrobe box being used as a prototype for the reference desk.

Figure 4.11.   The space before using a low-tech hologram.

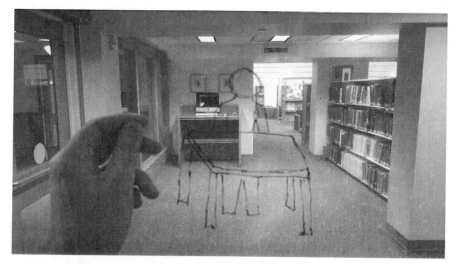

Figure 4.12. The space when viewed using a low-tech hologram, demonstrating the presence of a new service point.

Not all services involve physical objects or touchpoints. New services that do not involve a touchpoint also need to be prototyped. An experience can be prototyped by scripting, choreographing, and staging the service as if it were really happening. Questions for the research team to ask when staging a service experience are as follows: Did the user understand the service? Did the user understand the value of the service? Did the user understand how to use the service?[44] If the user can see the purpose, understand the value, and make sense of how to use it the prototyped service is a success. If any of the aforementioned three questions leave a user confounded, the research team should refine the prototype in response to user feedback.

Part of the prototyping process involves seeking feedback on the services the prototypes represent. Creating a feedback mechanism is easy. Common formats include creating online forms or sending e-mail requests to users. A convenient method that allows for users to be creative is the graffiti wall, which allows for crowdsourcing feedback at the point of the prototype. This easy-to-create feedback method involves hanging a large sheet of paper next to the prototype for users to provide contextual feedback. Figure 4.13 shows a graffiti wall for a website redesign project. We put a screenshot of the newly proposed homepage interface, along with paper for feedback, on a corkboard in the library lobby. The process was convenient and "encourages participation through natural means of facilitating casual, anonymous remarks."[45] It is also easy to set up and fun to read.

When?

Prototypes are tests of solutions and are best used near the end of the process. The best time might be near the end of the understanding/thinking phase and prior to implementation. Note that in the event the prototype doesn't pass the user test, this just means there is more work to be done. It does not indicate failure. Refine and refine again, but never give up.

Who?

The research team should be in charge, although prototyping might be a good exercise to work on with members of the UWG. The research team may or may not ask the UWG to help create a prototype. UWG members may want to help because they might enjoy building models, and their keen user perspective may help create a better prototype.

Materials?

Any materials that are available can be used to make prototypes. Paper, boxes, tape, or just about anything in a supply closet will work. We used a wardrobe box, and it worked well. It is okay to think outside the, er, wardrobe box on this one. Get creative and don't worry if it is imperfect or rough. The important thing is to help people see the possibilities.

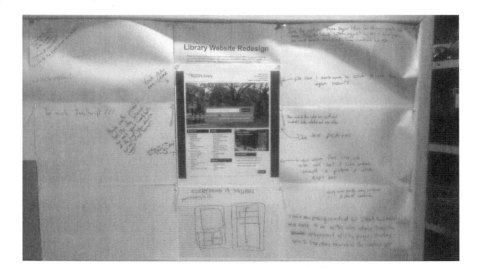

Figure 4.13.   The graffiti wall being used to solicit feedback on a homepage redesign.

ANALYSIS AND SYNTHESIS

What?

Analysis is the process of breaking larger chunks of data into smaller pieces. Synthesis is reassembling those smaller pieces into patterns.[46] By breaking up the data, laying it out, and moving concepts around, similar ideas can be grouped to see patterns and create insights.[47] Insights are built on themes and patterns detected during analysis.

Why?

The service design process is essentially an approach to gathering and collecting data with various exercises. To turn data into insights that can be used to design or improve services, it has to be analyzed and synthesized by the research team.

How?

There is no one best way to perform an analysis or synthesize the data. There are many different software packages available for synthesizing qualitative research. In this book, we do it the old-fashioned way, with pencils, sticky notes, and possibly a whiteboard. Software is convenient for large projects, but software or not, the research team should still meet to discuss and analyze the data. It is through the process of analysis and synthesis that the data inspires change.

Build a Wall

Move the data from a computer to a larger canvas, where the research team can see connections.[48] A wall is good because it allows the team to step back and see everything at once without having to lean over and potentially block a key comment.

Decontextualize

The data, whether it is in the form of transcriptions of audio recordings or notes taken during a discussion group, are linear reconstructions of an exchange between a user and members of the research team. Decontextualize the utterances—take those verbal snippets out of the linear transcription—to form patterns of thought. In nonlinear form, comments lose the identity associated with the speaker and become a voice of your users.

Reassemble and Create Patterns

The wall acts as a canvas for the sticky notes and enables the team to move them and group patterns.[49] This can be done by moving the sticky notes around, or even connecting them with lines or yarn. These patterns are what the research team will follow up on with the UWG in verbal discussion to confirm that the insights found are correct.

When?

Synthesis is best done during the understanding/thinking phase, although the team may want to evaluate data as it is received. Initial analysis sessions may help focus discussions between the research team and the UWG, to lead to greater insight and more focused solutions.

Who?

The research team is the main group involved in synthesis. It is not advisable to bring the UWG into the mix because they may not understand the process or the decontextualizing of the data, but the team should discuss the findings with the UWG to confirm the analysis.

Materials?

Analysis and synthesis can be carried out in a meeting or classroom space where the research team has access to a large wall or whiteboard to evaluate content.[50] Sticky notes, pens, and paper to write ideas on are also needed.

FOCUS GROUPS

What?

Focus groups are comprised of a number of users assembled to provide feedback on a product or service.[51] They typically consist of six to twelve participants and last about sixty to ninety minutes. Focus groups are highly structured, with carefully planned objectives and questions to guide the sessions.

Why?

The goal of a focus group is to evoke a reaction to an idea or concept to find out what users think about something. Focus groups are useful when the research team has specific ideas or possible changes they want to explore with users. While not the primary purpose of the focus group, the team will also often hear general impressions about the library, as well as answers to their specific questions. These findings should also be documented and shared with relevant administrators and staff members.

How?

The first step in running a focus group is deciding on the objective of the session, which should be guided by your research questions. The objective will help determine which user types to include, how long the session should last, and the types of questions to address. For example, our research team was exploring possible options for renovating our reference room when we decided we were ready to test some ideas with users. Our research questions were as follows: Why do students use the reference room now? Why don't they? What do they like/dislike about the reference room? What does a reference room for the future Reed College look like? What would encourage them to use reference services more?

After gathering substantial data from other exercises, our research team decided to have a focus group for first-year students with the objective of finding out what gets in the way of their using reference services and what changes would improve their experience in the reference room. The afore-mentioned questions provided the team with data, which was then turned into possible solutions. These were then brought to the focus group for a response. Because the focus group's participants were relatively inexperienced users, we decided to set the length of the session at 90 minutes so we would have time to take them on a tour prior to asking any questions.

Focus group participants should be users of the library. Student workers and volunteers cannot provide an accurate picture of how the average user feels about and uses the library. These groups can provide valuable information, but their experience is different from most users because they have inside information.

The next step is to develop a set of questions. You may want to ask the UWG to help develop the questions, format, and materials for the focus group. The UWG can inform the research team on these components, how library patrons may want to be addressed, and the order in which the questions should be asked. Developing a solid and focused script is an important element in conducting a focus group.[52] The script should include broad opening questions and required and optional follow-up questions organized in a set order. Practicing the questions with library staff or a small pilot focus group can help refine the script.

Once the script has been set, one member of the research team or the UWG should lead the focus group. A second team member may ask follow-up questions and other members take notes, but only one person should lead the conversation so as not to overwhelm or confuse participants. In addition to taking notes, audio or video should be used to record the focus group. It is ideal to have one to three team members to run the group and take notes. Having too many team members present may discourage participants from sharing.

When planning a focus group, the research team should consider how participants share answers in focus group settings. One known issue is that of dominant voices.[53] This happens when a participant says something and the group agrees with them because they do not want to look like dissenters. Focus group members also tend to alter their opinions because they want to get along with and be liked by others.[54] The leader of the group can work to lessen these issues by creating an inviting environment, using positive and inquisitive body language, encouraging participants to speak up, and letting participants know that all opinions are valuable and welcome.

When?

Focus groups are best held late in the understanding/thinking phase. In the service design process, focus groups are primarily used to provide opportunities for users to react to content and validate the findings of the research group, and not necessarily to introduce or gather new ideas.

Who?

The research team should organize, script, and run focus groups either alone or in collaboration with the UWG. Even if the UWG is not directly involved, their input on questions, format, and marketing is essential. The UWG may be able to help run the focus groups, but these groups are generally best run by members of the research team or someone trained in focus group facilitation.

Materials?

It is best for a focus group to meet in a space with a whiteboard or projector. Show visuals where possible to eliminate unnecessary confusion on the part of focus group participants. It is also important to provide some sort of incentive to participants for their time. This can be a small gift card or food at the session.

BLUEPRINTING

What?

The blueprint is a foundational document that outlines the underlying dependencies and requirements for a service. The blueprint shows both onstage (i.e., what the patron sees) and offstage (i.e., the systems and people needed to make a patron's task appear seamless) events and actions. It breaks steps down into their smallest components and "permits analysis, control, and improvement."[55]

Why?

Blueprints serve two functions. They are a visual record of how a service is performed and a method for making the intangible tangible.[56] Similar to architectural blueprints, the service blueprint is a reproduction of a design. In this case, how a service is performed is the design to be documented. The process for performing a service is often a product of unintentional design, and it exists as it does because different departments have cobbled together different workflows to create an overall process. Documenting the design provides a reference for how the service is performed. Blueprints are usually done later in the service design process because they provide a guide for how to ideally implement a service.

The second function of service blueprints is to make the intangible tangible. As in any system, altering timing or how a step is performed may result in a poor user experience. Highlighting pinch points or possible fail points during service delivery is an important part of the blueprint.[57] Many of the decisions that are made when someone uses a service happen in the user's mind. Finding out where people might get frustrated or where there are weaknesses in each step can help service providers see that "these processes are important, because changing them may alter the way consumers perceive the service."[58]

How?

The blueprint starts with another tool, the customer journey map (CJM). The research team should work closely with external users and internal stakeholders to formulate the internal (back end, or staff side) and external (front end, or user side) components in each step of the customer journey in the CJM. The research team documents the components, organizes them into a clear structure, and checks the structure to ensure accuracy.

As seen in figure 4.14, the steps in the user-action line are taken from a CJM of how to check out a book from reserves. It shows not only the onstage elements, but also the offstage ones. The line of interaction is the point of exchange between user and service provider. The items below the line of visibility are internal operations, and anything above that line is what the user sees, even if they may not interact with it directly. Above the user-action row is the physical evidence, which is where something happens (virtual, physical, in interaction with someone else, or alone). The stage is at the top of the blueprint and provides a visual grouping of similar tasks.

To create the blueprint, identify the stakeholders involved in each step of the CJM and decide how to get more input from them. You may want to interview, hold focus groups, conduct a survey, observe the service in action, or try another method to find out more about each step. The example mentioned earlier is very basic, providing a straightforward overview of checking out a book from reserves. You may choose to make a more complex blueprint that further breaks down one or more steps, depending on how you are planning to use it.

Whether you go into great detail or present a high-level view of the service, it is important to find a way to organize the blueprint so that the information is clear and the interconnections are highlighted. The research team may choose to do this after gathering information from users or stakeholders, or with the UWG or relevant library staff members. After creating the blueprint, it is crucial to get feedback on its contents and organization from those you worked with to create it. It is also important to get feedback from others who are invested in the process in some way, especially those who are involved with providing the service. Adjust the blueprint as appropriate in response to the feedback. The service blueprint should be consid-

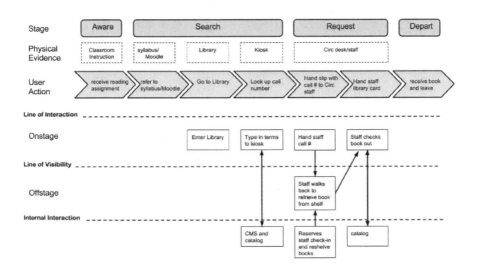

Figure 4.14. Blueprint of the steps required for a user to check out a book.

ered a living document that will change along with users, staff, technology, and resources.

When?

Service blueprints are created near the end of the understanding/thinking phase or during the implementation phase; however, they can also be made earlier as a method to document how tasks are currently being carried out. Blueprints of existing services can be used for analysis, while those created during the implementation phase are made for service innovation.[59] The blueprint process described here is meant to be carried out near the end of the research process.

Who?

The research team should work with as many stakeholders as possible, including users and members of the UWG, as well as internal stakeholders from the library staff. The research team must work closely with staff to understand how activities and tasks are performed internally, and with users to observe and discuss how they actually use the library.

Materials?

There is no set standard for making a blueprint, including materials that should be used. Sticky notes work well for arranging and rearranging elements with the many onstage and offstage players who should be represented. A wall or whiteboard can be helpful for sketching out the blueprint as a group. The final blueprint can be created in word processing, slideshow, or other software with simple flowchart and table capabilities.

SUMMARY

We've covered a lot of ground in this chapter. The tools in this section represent a portion of the tools currently being used by service designers throughout the world. This list is by no means exhaustive, but is more of a representation of the various methods available. We recommend choosing the tools that work best for your research. In the next chapter, we review how to adapt the service design methodology to your library. Adapting the tools and knowing when to use them is one of the best ways to get the most out of your research and give focus to your own efforts in your library.

Chapter Five

Adapting Service Design to Your Library

So far in this book, we've discussed how services work in libraries and the role service design can play when developing or improving them. We've presented tools and examples from the service design toolkit, but we have not provided a garden path for exactly how to produce your own service design project. Because service design is an extremely malleable methodology that scales up or down and is highly contextual, you should craft your own project based on your specific needs. In this chapter, we look more closely at how to do just that.

CREATING EFFICIENT IN-HOUSE TEAMS

The basic roles and functions of in-house teams. In this chapter, we focus on the soft skills that make good research teammates. Like any skill, many of these can be learned, but some people bring these talents with them at the outset, which can be highly beneficial when working with a tight timeline. People can learn additional usability and user-experience skills much more quickly and easily than the soft skills necessary to be part of a good research team. We discuss these qualities in more detail in the following sections.

Communication

Members of a research team not only need to be able to talk to one another, but also listen. This seems like such an obvious skill for a team, but too often we see examples (and we're sure you have seen this in your own experience) where the ability to communicate was left out of the mix when forming teams. For our purposes, communication is the ability to effectively ex-change information in a timely manner in the method that makes the most sense for the given message. When doing service design work, good communication between team members, users, staff members, and other stakeholders is essential.

Functional Expertise

Look for people who have either the skills or the aptitude for user research. The skills and mindset required to execute a service design project can be learned, but it will be helpful if at least some of your team members have a background in usability or user testing. Moreover, try to find staff members who have the different types of experience or expertise you need to help move your project forward. For example, if you are working on a project to explore service desks in the library, it will be helpful to have at least one person who actually works at the desks. It is also a good idea to look for members with complementary skills.

Team Players

Team members should be able to work well with others and put the mission before disagreements. When there is a disagreement, members need to be able to settle the issue so they can move on. Members should be willing to speak up when they disagree but do so courteously. Dissent can bring positive results when delivered appropriately.

Experimentation and Learning

A desire to learn and a willingness to be wrong are great assets for members of your team to possess. Having team members who are open-minded, ask lots of questions, and are willing to take risks will allow the team members to thoroughly test ideas. Service design has a strong exploratory component. Thus, team members need to be curious and comfortable with ambiguity.

Critical Thinking and Problem Solving

You will need critical thinkers and problem solvers on your team. Service design studies produce a lot of data, so you should look for people who can dissect it to make sense of the information gathered. These people are good at seeing patterns in the fog of data. Critical thinking not only helps when synthesizing findings, but also in creating solutions based on them. The critical thinker applies levelheaded contemplation to help distinguish something "cool" from something practical and long-lasting. It is not necessary to have an experienced data analyst on your team, especially since we are not doing intensive quantitative analysis. Team members can bring their ideas together to analyze the data. In addition, combining diverse staff perspectives when looking at the data will push the critical-thinking and problem-solving power of your team even further.

Diverse Perspectives

Diversity adds depth to any service design team. Try to have different perspectives represented on the team. By assembling the research team using people from the different library departments, the team will naturally achieve a diversity of perspectives when approaching an idea. Divergent staff perspectives provide a depth that will be lacking if all team members are from a single department or division. Different perspectives provide the team with the ability to see the various facets of any situation and will allow members to think beyond their silos. Another reason to have team members from different departments is their ability to speak the language of their division. This will also be important when the team needs to share information on project updates with the various divisions of the library.

Big-Picture Thinking

Too often we are unable to see beyond our own departmental silo. Members of the research team are staff members who can see the forest for the trees. They have the ability to see the micro and macro elements in the organization. They can see what impacts their own work as it pertains to their departmental mission, but also the bigger picture of how the various departments are tightly coupled to deliver library services. Big-picture thinkers are able to see beyond the immediate and understand that tweaking an internal process may affect another department's work. They are systems thinkers who bring their "sight" to the research team. This skill is invaluable to service design.

ASSEMBLING A USER WORKING GROUP

A key component to the service design process is the user working group (UWG). This group is comprised of library users who are interested in moving the library forward. The research team will work closely with the UWG to understand user behavior and motivation. The UWG will help decipher and uncover meaning behind behavior. It functions as a bridge between library staff and library users. They are both primary respondents to ideas and findings, and the research team's personal guides to the users. Because they are in a position to influence future decision making in the library, it is important that the research team vet the UWG members and find those users who are truly invested in the well-being of the library and its mission.

So how do you get users to not only provide feedback, but also stay engaged in the process? There is no easy answer. The first step is to reach out to users using the methods that have proven to be most effective for other types of programming. This may be in the form of fliers, e-mail, electronic (or paper) newsletters, social media, or word of mouth. You may also want to go to city or student council meetings or the Friends of the Library association and ask for recommendations. Personal referrals are also a reliable method for getting interested patrons to join the UWG. Patrons befriend librarians all the time. Using those connections has been one of our most successful methods for finding highly engaged members.

Small incentives can also help. If you have the budget, feed the UWG for their time. Good UWG members are involved because they are interested in the process and want to have a say in what happens to the library. But it is a nice gesture to offer participants snacks or coffee because it lets them know you appreciate their time. Some students are required to complete a certain number of community service hours for a course or scholarship. If you work at a college or university, letting the community service or scholarship office know about opportunities can help you locate volunteers who have an extra incentive for getting and staying involved.

We recommend that you avoid approaching student workers or volunteers about being on the UWG. They have had a behind-the-scenes look at the inner workings of the library and may know too much about internal processes. Their inside information may create a bias and influence their responses or make it hard for them to separate their staff knowledge from their user knowledge. It is still important to get input from these groups, but it should be part of gathering information among internal stakeholders.

When creating the UWG, focus on the end goal. If looking at resources tailored to a subset of the user population, make sure members of that specific subset are included. The UWG should reflect the goal of the project. If you are planning a broader project focused on general usage, try to get individuals who can represent most library patrons. This might include equal parts men and women, but also look at ethnicity and race, occupation (if it might influence how the library is used), age, and other characteristics that might be important in your user group.

What Was Your Motivation to Be Part of the User Working Group and Eventually the Library User Experience Team
By Emma Williams-Baron

As I started to think about why I joined the user working group, my first instinct was that I joined because of my strong emotional attachment to the library. But then I remembered that I had seen the posters asking for participants and decided not to join because of the time commitment. In fact, I had originally consciously chosen not to join. Then, as I was walking through the library one day, one of the librarians approached me. I had never spoken to her before but had seen her in the library several times. She told me she had seen me in the library frequently, too, and asked me to join the user working group. Faced with a personal invitation, and flattered that someone had noticed I spent a lot of time in the library, I agreed. And the promise of free food also helped!

Once I joined the group, I became interested in the project. The process was fun—I liked being asked questions and having my answers valued, and feeling like I had some input in changing the library. And I had strong feelings about the library: I spent a lot of my time there, which meant it was central to my identity, and I got to know small irritations very well because I encountered them every day. Furthermore, after meeting several times, our group began to develop good rapport, making it a more enjoyable experience and a nice break from studying. As I got more involved, I felt more tied to the library, which tied me closer to the project. When the librarians asked us to join the Library User Experience team, I was happy to do so, because I was engaged in the mission of the project and wanted to see what it was like to run a focus group.

So, my motivations for participating in the project were numerous: I was personally invited; I was emotionally tied to the library; the process was flattering and empowering; our group developed good rapport; free food meant I didn't have to leave for a meal, so I could do more work in the library; I became invested in the mission and felt a certain sense of ownership in the project; and I got to develop new skills. I have been pleased to watch the project grow and am proud of the changes planned and those already made!

MAINTAINING OPENNESS AND TRANSPARENCY

Nothing will impede the work of a research team more than a lack of trust among other staff members. Make a serious effort to share what you learn. Do not make changes without additional consultation or sharing with colleagues. Be open and transparent. The work of the research team is about enhancing the service delivery model of the library and should not be seen as a boost to a single department. Nor should a single department get credit for the work being done by the research team. The efforts of the team will hopefully be seen as working toward process improvement for the whole library.

You will want support for your project from administration and staff members. Because most projects that deal with service improvement are generated from the top rather than the bottom, administrative buy-in may already be a given. Suggest to the library director or administrator in charge of approving the project that the team's efforts be shared with the rest of the library. Sharing in an all-staff meeting or via e-mail will also provide the umph your project may need to demonstrate the support it carries. A public blessing can build credibility with coworkers.

There will likely be many questions from library staff members about the research team's work. Communicating what the team is not doing with people who are not part of the team is as powerful a tool as informing library staff of what the team is doing.[1] The research team should provide periodic updates at library division meetings, as well as e-mails to all staff. Team members are responsible for regularly sharing information about the team's work with their department or division. The chair of the research team should also make themselves available to answer any questions, either via e-mail or in one-on-one meetings. You cannot share too much about the project in general, but never share anything not about specific patrons or users. Part of the trust that the research team builds with the UWG or in user focus groups comes from the promise of confidentiality. The best way to ensure that you follow through on that promise is to create a protocol for how audio recordings and notes from the UWG meetings are stored and handled. It is good practice to have participants agree to be recorded for the sole purpose of creating insights representative of users in general. Generalize what was heard from users to protect the individuals who shared that information. If you work in higher education, consult with your Institutional Review Board to determine if you need their approval for the project.

UNDERSTANDING YOUR CONTEXT
(AND WHY YOUR LIBRARY IS UNIQUE)

In chapter 2, we wrote about context as the backdrop for services and how that backdrop is a key factor in how services are performed. In this chapter, we look at context in architectural terms. *Inside* refers to those bits and pieces the library controls that the user considers to be part of the library and the library experience, while *outside* refers to those things that are not controlled by the library or part of the user's library experience.[2] The library's physical footprint creates a boundary that helps the user delineate the literal outside from the inside, but as we look closer at what makes up context, we will broaden the concept of context to include four areas: 1) internal environment, 2) built environment, 3) touchpoint locations, and 4) external environment.

Context extends beyond the walls of the library to encompass not only the library, but also the system of which the library is a part. Context is also about the physical and cultural elements that impact how service providers and users engage with the space and the services provided within.[3] In an academic library, this will include the campus(es) your library serves. For a public library, this will include the greater county, town, or city that your library serves. These greater levels of context can influence what happens inside the library without us knowing it. In this section, we review context and the various levels of context you should understand before starting your project.

Internal Environment

The internal environment is what your library looks and feels like from the inside—not what the building looks like (discussed in the next section on built environment), but what it feels like in meetings and while working at service desks. Are these feelings on display for patrons to see and experience? If the feelings are negative, do they impact the user experience? Culture includes the shared and accepted feelings and assumptions[4] that build throughout time and become lodged in the collective employee psyche. Does your library's culture focus on service delivery? It not, why?

Culture is hard to change. Changing your culture to be something that it is not is like getting a brontosaurus to pivot on a dime.[5] Culture lumbers and creeps. While you may not be able to change culture, you can assess[6] the general assumptions upheld by the library culture and use them to your advantage to understand their influence on the library's service delivery model. Organizational culture is similar to inherited ecology. It is something that builds throughout time to the point where assumptions are accepted as fact and become the reason behind such responses as, "That is how we do things here" or "We tried that once and it did not work." It is important to understand those assumptions to get a sense of how they influence the service experience and work toward changing or adapting those bits and pieces to produce optimal user experiences.

Built Environment

The built environment is the physical building. As the setting for your services, the built library should accentuate the collection, space usage, and the various services. A library's physical presence is felt in everything we do. We can't separate "library" as a concept and a series of services aimed at specific populations from "library" the building that houses the books. The library acts as a "stage setting that prompts visitors to enact a performance of some kind, whether or not actual visitors would describe it as such (and whether or not they are prepared to do so). From this perspective, [libraries] appear as environments structured around specific ritual scenarios."[7] Knowing about the rituals is one part of understanding; the other is how the physical library impacts and influences those rituals and how they are performed.

At times you may find that the built environment is not working as it should. Perhaps the architect designed something they wanted to create and ended up hiding the riches of the library behind the "dishonest mask of pretended order."[8] Or maybe you are just dealing with an older building that does not easily work with current technology. By looking closely at how patrons move throughout the building, the research team may feel that simply rearranging the contents will make spaces work better. Consider the examples in figures 5.1–5.4.

In figure 5.1, a user is sitting at a table using a laptop. A table is the perfect service for using a laptop, writing in a notebook, or stacking books waiting to be read. But figure 5.2 shows that the user could not find easy access to an outlet from the table. This might be an oversight by the architect or whoever installed the shelving units. Luckily, the student was creative and found a way to overcome the hurdle by running the power cord through the shelf unit.

Figure 5.1.   A user sitting at a table using a laptop with the laptop plugged in.

Figure 5.2. A user sitting at a table using a laptop with the power cord draped through stacks to reach an outlet.

The students in figures 5.3 and 5.4 have adapted flat or angled surfaces to accommodate their preference to stand while working. Every surface, square foot of carpet, table, and chair can potentially be modified to become something it was not originally intended to be. By attending to the built environment, you can identify where things are working, where things are not working, and where to make improvements.

Figure 5.3. A user adapting a flat surface to make a standing desk.

Figure 5.4.   A user adapting a slanted surface to make a standing desk.

Touchpoint Locations

An extension of the built environment is touchpoint locations and design. We are often stuck with service desks that were put in place long ago to respond to different users and needs (see figure 5.5). Predicting the future is always difficult, but rapid technology changes have made it even more difficult during the past twenty years. This issue can be especially problematic for touchpoint design. You may be dealing with multiple entrances to the library, inflexible desks sculpted to add presence and weight to a touchpoint, too many service desks, or other legacies inherited from previous times. Investigating how current patrons work and talking with them about what they expect from the future can help us update touchpoints.

Figure 5.5.   Predicting the future is hard. Here we see a former media desk shuttered due to an unforeseen change in how patrons consume media.

External Environment

Where does your library call home? Are you at a public library that is part of a larger county or city system? Or an academic library on a small liberal arts college campus or in a large statewide system? Understanding the outside forces that influence how work is done inside your library is a major part of context. The outside forces may not just be conceptual or physical. Some external forces to consider are listed here, but there are likely many more that will impact your specific library.

Proximity to Other Public Services

What other services are located near your library? Do those services impact you or vice versa? Should you be sharing information with one another to better serve users? Are your services clearly stated on your website or in handouts to try to limit user confusion? Think about this from the user's perspective.

Parking and Public Transportation

Is there enough parking or ease of access to public transportation? How do patrons arrive and depart from the library? If in an urban setting, are there enough bike racks or a space for a short-term car rental? Do you have directions to parking and public transportation on your website?

Access to the Building

Are there ramps leading to the front door? If there is the need for wheelchair access, is the access point in a visible spot that is easily accessible from public transit or the parking lot? Is it well marked? Once inside the building, can users navigate and access the majority of the collection without assistance?

Curriculum and Other Relevant Educational Programming

For academic librarians, the curriculum of the college or university impacts all aspects of your work. Based on the type of institution the library serves, a different curriculum and the absence or presence of graduate students will change the environment and the focus. Likewise, public libraries offer programs based on the curriculum of nearby schools. Going even further, knowing where there are gaps in services offered in support of educational programs can help when developing services. For example, your library may want to offer tutoring, specialized software, focused collections, group study spaces just for high school students, or other services in response to educational needs in the community.

OWNING SERVICE DESIGN

Your job as a member of your library's user experience or research team is to learn how *your* library operates. Step outside your comfort zone and away from the organization chart and explore. Work someone else's job or ask them a lot of questions about what they do each day. Work like a student or a patron in the library and away from your office. Use their bathrooms, find books like they do, and ask lots of questions. See how your library ticks and create your team and your approach to learning how services are consumed. This in-depth, applied ethnographic approach will demonstrate how the library really works from the user's perspective. It will also give insight into how the patrons see the library. If you are leading a service design project, you should do this before putting your team together and continuously throughout the project. If you are a member of a user experience or research team, you should also spend time thinking and working like a user. Owning your project and your library will help you do the immersive work necessary for a successful service design project.

Bibliothecarius Habilis

Use the tools in this book, but adapt them to your environment. You need not use all the tools, but pick a few and tailor them to the project and the context. Perhaps prototypes are frowned upon in your library. You can get past this by creating a hologram in sketching software. Perhaps you want to find out why users choose specific places to work, but you have a very quiet library and cannot talk to users as they work. You may decide to do a short tabletop survey to obtain this information rather than contextual interviews. In short, use this book as it best suits your needs.

Don't Blindly Follow Trends

Reading about trends is good, but before implementing a trend you should research your own environment. Service design provides a thought-provoking platform that is solution agnostic. The service design research team should work to develop a mindset that avoids preconceived notions, is open, and leads to powerful shared experiences as it honestly seeks to learn more about how patrons use resources. This may result in the team recommending that the library adopt a hot trend, but it is important to make sure that user and staff needs and expectations, as well as the context in which they happen, are attended to first.

SUMMARY

- Libraries usually don't have the luxury of hiring big-name consulting firms, and even if they did, creating an in-house team may be the best option. Service design is not difficult to do, but there are some key ingredients in creating your in-house research team. Team members should have the ability to communicate and work well with others. They should have some level of functional expertise and knowledge of basic user experience tools. The individuals on the team should be team players and have the ability to put the team mission before personal matters. Members should possess a willingness to experiment (and, at times, be wrong). The team should consist of people from different library divisions. Team members should have the ability to see the big picture.
- Too often libraries create teams to work on projects, but they don't share what they are working on. Openness will go a long way in assuaging the fears of those who are not part of the team about what the team is doing. Communicating what the team *is not* doing is as important as communicating what the team *is* doing.
- Understanding the context in which your library operates fosters a better understanding of the library's place in the greater ecology. Context is more than just setting. It includes internal environment, the built environment, touchpoint locations, and external environment. Being cognizant of context allows the research team to tailor its efforts to the project at hand and own service design. Owning it means adapting it to your environment and your context.

Chapter Six

Looking Forward

Too often in libraries, assessment projects are started with a "this will only happen once" mindset, with little thought about what will happen after the project ends. Teams are created, methodologies are learned, solutions are implemented, and then life returns to normal after the process is complete; however, just thinking about the costs associated with planning and implementing a project shows how shortsighted that type of thinking can be. Holding meetings, planning, training, learning, analyzing, and implementing solutions require a significant amount of time and resources. In this chapter, we discuss what should happen after your project ends, argue for the need to create a culture of ongoing and meaningful assessment, explain how to maintain an in-house research team, and discuss what we believe should be the next steps for service design in libraries.

CREATING A CULTURE OF ONGOING ASSESSMENT

Creating a culture of assessment reinforces the idea that there are many moving parts that need to work together effectively in any organization. Libraries are user-centered, user-serving, and user-funded institutions; therefore, we have a responsibility to ensure that we are good stewards of the resources we manage. For some, this may require altering how you think about doing your job. For most, it requires becoming more mindful of how we operate as a collective organism. As a system of tightly coupled departments, libraries benefit from ongoing assessment because it helps make efforts transparent to all library staff by emphasizing the service delivery model and the user experience.

What Assessment Is (and Is Not)

Assessment isn't just about taking the temperature of a service at a given point in time. It is about ongoing monitoring of the service. Assessment done at a given time only tells you what is happening at that time. Ongoing, longitudinal efforts can help identify trends in how services are consumed and changes in how users interact with a service, which may point to a fundamental shift in user behavior. That larger fundamental shift may suggest a need to adjust how services are rendered to better satisfy current user needs and expectations. This kind of information can only be revealed through ongoing assessment, rather than piecemeal, project-based approaches.

Ongoing Assessment

Ongoing assessment is about creating a culture of assessment. Organizationally, this means looking at assessment as a regular work-related task, so that it is something we regularly do[1] and not part of "other duties as assigned." Creating ongoing assessment emphasizes strategic thinking so that it permeates the efforts of all those involved in service delivery. If everyone is considered with how the service is performed, is consumed, and can be improved, the entire library will be involved and invested in ushering in change so that staff are constantly evolving alongside patrons. Creating a culture of assessment also contributes to practicing mindful librarianship, which is being aware of what you are doing and how you are doing it so that you are fully engaged in your work.

To a certain extent, ongoing assessment is already part of most libraries. Your library probably already keeps circulation statistics and gate counts. The reference desk probably tracks questions in a database. The web librarian may periodically share page views of the library's website. The instruction librarians are probably assessing their classes. And every library has extensive collection usage data. These are all forms of ongoing assessment, but it is likely that these are not being shared outside the department doing the assessment. In addition, the data is not often used as fully as it could be to help staff reflect on changes in user behavior and as feeder information for developing questions about users that could be explored more thoroughly with other data collection methods. This type of data also does a poor job of assessing how changes to services have impacted users.

Creating a Plan

The previous examples are usually contained in silos. Circulation stats and gate counts might only be shared between access services and the library director. Web page data might only be shared between the web librarian and the rest of the IT contingent. Reference and instruction statistics are only shared among the reference and instruction librarians. This great information is less useful if only shared with a few people. Ongoing assessment means sharing the results and efforts to look for redundancy that can be eliminated and consolidated, and to find data points that enhance one another.

For example, in our own space-usage study, we performed floor sweeps of the entire building two weeks out of every semester every hour that the reference desk was open, including capturing gate counts for those same times. If our access services department had also been gathering gate counts at the same time, we could have increased efficiency by asking for that data rather than integrating gate counts into the sweep activities. We could have enhanced our findings further if we had also captured page-view counts, database search counts, and reference interactions for the times we did building counts. This would have provided us with a fuller picture of user activity, providing a nice snapshot of how the library is used at different times.

Getting different perspectives during the data gathering phase may help develop fresh understandings about seemingly routine tasks. As you work to create a culture of assessment, talk with other staff about data gathering methods and data that already exists. You might find better methods for capturing data or even that there are parts of the service workflow that you understand much better only after talking about how to gather data about it. You may also discover that staff want to be more informed about assessment efforts and results, and would like a shared, library-wide dashboard to display the data so it can be used by everyone. The only way to really find out is to ask and be inclusive.

One way to reinforce the idea that assessment is part of the culture is to make a master plan of assessment for the entire library. The aforementioned examples are standard statistics kept in libraries, but the next step is to track patron satisfaction, usage, and behavior. This is best done with a more detailed plan and maybe the creation of a dedicated research or assessment team. Moreover, at some point, an annual report will probably be due to some higher entity. If you work in a siloed library, the cobbling together of usage statistics is a nightmare, with high costs. Creating a library-wide assessment plan allows for ease of consolidation throughout library divisions. A library-wide assessment plan is simply an outline of what efforts the library will track and who is responsible for each. The level of detail for the plan will depend on the library's size and commitment to assessment, as well as how the plan is going to be used. Sometimes a spreadsheet listing the four major components of an assessment plan is enough. These include activities, goals, assessment measures, and stakeholders. If more detail is needed, start with the four components and build your plan with the other elements you need added in.

Service design and the research team can take the front seat when developing an assessment plan for the entire library because they can reinforce the notion that you are trying to develop a holistic view of the overall library and its service delivery; however, it is important to note that the data gathered using this method is not greater than the more traditional data already being gathered. Together, they create the big picture of what the library really looks like and how it is used. We are calling for a more unified effort throughout all departments to consolidate and organize assessment efforts and make assessment a more open and transparent process that pervades all aspects of the library and throughout all staff members and their divisions. When those efforts are codified, the next logical step is to consolidate the data in a single place. An online dashboard or a periodic internal newsletter can also help solidify and reinforce the importance of continuous assessment.

Reflexivity

Assessment is also about reflexivity. While the majority of your service design efforts will involve measuring and analyzing usage by patrons, we also need to keep an eye on ourselves. The user's experience is only as good as the service being offered and the people offering it. While looking outward, we should also look inward at our own service delivery. At some point, the research team will want to make a service blueprint (see chapter 4 for more details). This blueprint can help staff keep a watchful eye on how a service is being performed. Any changes in how a service is being performed should be reflected in the blueprint, which serves as both a model for how to perform a service and an instrument to measure efficacy of a service. Turning the tables and looking at how we actually deliver services allows us to learn about the internal user experience as well. Service design is about the experience from the service provider's perspective, as well as that of the user. Seeing one or the other is not seeing the entire picture.

Assessment Is Fun (Yeah, You Read That Correctly)

Assessment is fun. There we said it. And it's true. Measuring usage is (or can be) fun. It might not be as fun as riding a sled down a hill covered in fresh snow, but it is fun nonetheless. It is fun in the sense that we are learning about our own library, how our efforts are appreciated, and how we can improve lives by helping users find a specific book or resource that helps answer their research question, learn a new hobby or skill, or simply provide pleasure. Making the effort to reach out and talk to users, and get their honest feedback, through conversation is uplifting. It allows us to make connections with the people we work for and justifies our efforts.

Assessment can be as simple as making hash marks on a piece of paper, but it can also mean making human connections with users. Too often librarians fear assessment because it can seem overwhelming and scary. But we can also take a less rigid interpretation and make assessment an ongoing conversation with patrons. It can mean simply being more observant and asking the occasional "Why do they do that?" and then sharing that question and observation with colleagues. When we know who our users are, why they do what they do, and what makes them human, we can work toward creating the optimal experience for them every time they use the library.

MAINTAINING YOUR IN-HOUSE SERVICE DESIGN TEAM

Creating a research team helps solidify the assessment efforts of any library. The presence of the team alone emphasizes the importance of assessment as part of the library's normal operations and mission. Creating the research team is relatively easy. The next step is making them part of ongoing assessment in the library. This section focuses on the ongoing use of the team and how to help them be successful.

Consistency (Small Is Pretty Big)

Making assessment a consistent part of the cultural fabric of your library will be easier if you keep the team together. The research team is made up of members from the various divisions in the library for two reasons: Team members provide perspective learned in their own divisions and a line of communication between their divisions and the research team. Having a small group of staff members lead assessment efforts guarantees consistency and helps ensure that all divisions will be informed about and involved in the process. Making team membership a long-term commitment can also be beneficial as the team figures out how to operate and work together, and the skills they will learn are not necessarily easily picked up by new members. The unified effort of the research team will benefit the library in the end and create a more consistent level of user experience.

It may be helpful to add additional team members on a temporary basis as new skills or people are required to gather data or perform certain user experience-related functions. Keeping the group small makes it more nimble (and easier to schedule meetings and events). It also makes it easier to get group members up to speed on new techniques to use when gathering data. Maintaining a research team is not without its costs. Any minute spent doing assessment is a minute not spent elsewhere. But if assessment is part of the culture of the library, overall costs are minimized by sharing the work across the team and by eliminating redundancy. Moreover, maintaining the team reduces costs related to starting a new research team.

New Projects

After completing its first service design project, the team can take project requests from other departments within the library. Because the team will have already learned how to operate, it will be in the position to lend its services to divisions throughout the library. It will also be more familiar with service design and other types of assessment methodologies. Thus, it can spend its research time focusing on learning about the project and the research goals, and not learning a methodology. The more the team works together, the better it will function. Not only will it be more efficient, but it will also function more like an actual team, through a focus on research goals.

Research teams may end up with requests for new projects, or they may need to create their own. Either way, when taking on a new project, the team must remember the importance of choosing a methodology based on the questions being asked and the information needed. Hopefully, everyone on the team is excited about service design. As a flexible methodology and set of tools, it can be adapted to most user studies, but it is still important to verify this with prework and discussion. In addition, it is important to carefully select a tool based on what you want to find out, rather than trying to make a tool or method fit the question.

SERVICE DESIGN AS A FUTURE OF LIBRARY ASSESSMENT

Service design is an all-encompassing, powerful, and empowering assessment methodology. We've all been to conferences or read articles about what another library is doing to better understand their patrons. Imagine being so excited about what you've learned that you go home from a conference and begin working on a plan to integrate the methodology into your own library because it worked perfectly for another facility. You get buy-in and create your team. You learn all you can about the methodology, and your project works great. You get a gold star for your efforts, but with the project complete, it is time to get back to your "old" job. So while the gold star hangs on your wall, the impact of the newly learned method lies dormant.

Service design can bridge that gap, making library assessment ongoing and manageable, resulting in a continuous feedback loop that leads to action. Due to its flexible nature and scalability, services can be used to not only assess service delivery, but also understand how users navigate the library across channels. It can show us the importance of mirroring the physical library and online user interfaces in response to how users use devices to help navigate the stacks, find ejournals, check library accounts, order from ILL, and so on.

Libraries, like most work environments, are siloed. People do not usually think far beyond their immediate branch on the organization chart. Immediate concerns tend to be limited to the departments and only on other departments if time permits or if you develop an interest for some reason. Service design reinforces the importance of seeing the forest for the trees and truly understanding the interdependencies that exist and are built into library systems. It hinges on systems thinking and the ability to see connections. This ability is what we have been waiting for in libraries (or any environment, for that matter). We may not all be in the business of assessment, but this methodology has the power to make it part of library culture so that assessment and assessment thinking are at the forefront, allowing library staff to integrate it into their daily work. As assessment becomes part of the library's cultural fabric, it becomes more than just another task with defined time parameters. And as it becomes the norm and part of what libraries do, users will have a better experience using library resources.

We promote the idea of creating a research team to address individual projects. But there are three things mentioned in this book that can be actively promoted in all libraries to change how we conduct ourselves and get the library more in line with service design thinking: adopting the service design mindset, embracing the top-down initiative of continuous assessment, and looking at everything as a service.

The service design mindset is about thinking in systems and seeing the tightly coupled nature of the library and its various components. The top-down initiative of continuous assessment means thinking that there is always room to improve, refine, and revision. This doesn't mean always looking for fault, but rather being aware of changes in user behavior and mindful that the library has to adapt to that change. Finally, by looking at everything as a service, librarians recognize that everything their library offers should and does have meaning to users. If a library were just a storehouse for books, we would only need a drive-thru window. But we do so much more than just hand books over to patrons. Everything we offer is a service. The sooner we realize this, the sooner we will begin to think like a user and put them in the center of all that we do.

Altering your way of thinking using these three concepts gets at the heart of what we have discussed in this book. Service design as a mindset can only really be appreciated when it is accepted as a viable method for assessment. When library workers begin to work as a team, with users as the focus, we can not only create a more optimal experience for users, but also get the entire library working as a cohesive unit. As more staff members feel they are part of a living organism, they'll feel obligated to provide feedback and become more invested in their work. As we all become more invested in our work, we can focus on delivering the best service for our users.

SUMMARY

Creating a culture of ongoing assessment is about making assessment part of the cultural fabric of the library. Ongoing assessment gives the library a longitudinal view of how patrons use its resources. Creating an assessment culture begins with making an overall plan for how and when assessment is done. This longitudinal view is beneficial to planning and budgeting, as well as getting more staff involved in connecting the library's mission to its daily work. And assessment can be fun. Yes, we said it can be fun.

- Librarians think in terms of projects. A component of creating an ongoing assessment culture is maintaining an in-house research team. The benefits of maintaining an in-house team are consistency, teamwork, and cost savings. The team will learn to work together and be on solid footing when it comes to understanding and implementing a user experience methodology, so there is no need to waste time getting people up to speed. One method to keep the team together is to have them take requests from library divisions in need of user testing. This not only keeps the team active, but also helps members learn more about the library through exposure to the inner workings of the various library units.
- Service design is a powerful, malleable assessment methodology. Given its ability to scale and provide a holistic view of the library as a system of systems, service design could be the future of library assessment. If nothing else, the service design mindset gives library user experience professionals the tools to look more closely at how a library works from a user-centered perspective.
- Service design can be broken down into three concepts: adopting a service design mindset, maintaining a top-down initiative of continuous assessment, and looking at everything as a service. Implementing the service design mindset allows the research team to focus on the user and be more empathetic toward their experience. Using a top-down initiative of continuous assessment is about making assessment something we do. And all library offerings are services for our patrons. The quicker we understand this, the quicker we can focus on the user's needs to create the optimal experience.

Notes

1. THE CASE FOR SERVICE DESIGN IN LIBRARIES, OR LIBRARIES AS SYSTEMS

1. Henry Dreyfuss, "The Industrial Designer and the Businessman," *Harvard Business Review* 28, no. 6 (November 1950): 80.

2. Tim Brown, *Change by Design: How Design Thinking Transforms Organizations and Inspires Innovation* (New York: Harper Business, 2009), 178.

3. Not all library services are consumed in the physical library. The library's website may be accessed from a mobile device via the device browser or an app. In this case, "context" could be just about anywhere. Understanding when and how needs arise is our job as library user experience researchers.

4. Donella H. Meadows, *Thinking in Systems: A Primer* (White River Junction, Vt.: Chelsea Green, 2008), 11.

5. Peter M. Senge, *The Fifth Discipline: The Art and Practice of the Learning Organization*, rev. and updated ed. (New York: Doubleday/Currency, 2006), 3.

6. Genevieve Bell and Joseph Kaye, "Designing Technology for Domestic Spaces: A Kitchen Manifesto," *Gastronomica: The Journal of Food and Culture* 2, no. 2 (May 2002): 46–62, doi:10.1525/gfc.2002.2.2.46; Joe Marquez and Annie Downey, "Service Design: An Introduction to a Holistic Assessment Methodology of Library Services," *Weave: Journal of Library User Experience* 1, no. 2 (2015), doi:http://dx.doi.org/10.3998/weave.12535642.0001.201.

7. Frederick Taylor, *The Principles of Scientific Management* (New York: Harper & Brothers, 1911).

8. Meadows, *Thinking in Systems*, 2.

9. Meadows, *Thinking in Systems*.

10. Meadows, *Thinking in Systems*, 14.

11. Christopher Meyer and Andre Schwager, "Understanding Customer Experience," *Harvard Business Review* 85, no. 2 (February 2007): 118.

12. Donald A. Norman, "The Way I See It: Systems Thinking: A Product Is More Than the Product," *Interactions* 16, no. 5 (September 2009): 52–54, doi:10.1145/1572626.1572637.

13. Andrew Polaine, "Designing for Services beyond the Screen," *A List Apart*, June 25, 2013, http://alistapart.com/article/designing-for-services-beyond-the-screen .

14. Peter Morville, *Intertwingled: Information Changes Everything* (Ann Arbor, Mich.: Semantic Studios, 2014), 15.

15. Clifford Geertz, "The Bazaar Economy: Information and Search in Peasant Marketing," *American Economic Review* 68, no. 2 (May 1978): 29.

16. Clayton M. Christensen and Michael E. Raynor, *The Innovator's Solution: Creating and Sustaining Successful Growth* (Boston: Harvard Business Review Press, 2013): 79.

17. Meyer and Schwager, "Understanding Customer Experience."

18. Livework Intelligence, "How People Cluster Experiences in Their Life," *Livework*, October 21, 2015, http://liveworkstudio.com/intelligence/how-people-cluster-experiences-in-their-life/.

19. Yi-Fu Tuan, *Space and Place: The Perspective of Experience* (Minneapolis: University of Minnesota Press, 1989).

20. Daniel R. Williams and Jerry J. Vaske, "The Measurement of Place Attachment: Validity and Generalizability of a Psychometric Approach," *Forest Science* 49, no. 6 (2003): 831.

21. Williams and Vaske, "The Measurement of Place Attachment," 831.

22. Williams and Vaske, "The Measurement of Place Attachment"; Tuan, *Space and Place*.

23. Joe Marquez, Annie Downey, and Ryan Clement, "Walking a Mile in the User's Shoes: Customer Journey Mapping as a Method to Understanding the User Experience," *Internet Reference Services Quarterly* 20, no. 3/4 (2015): 135–50, doi:10.1080/10875301.2015.1107000.

24. Bell and Kaye, "Designing Technology for Domestic Spaces."

25. Genevieve Bell, "Making Sense of Museums: The Museum as 'Cultural Ecology,'" *Intel Labs* 1 (2002): 4.

26. Morville, *Intertwingled*, 64.

27. Arnold van Gennep, *The Rites of Passage*, trans. Monika B. Vizedom and Gabrielle L. Caffee (Chicago: University of Chicago Press, 2001).

28. Victor W. Turner, *The Ritual Process: Structure and Anti-Structure*. Symbol, Myth, and Ritual Series (Ithaca, N.Y: Cornell University Press, 1977), 95.

29. Erica L. Wagner, Sue Newell, and William Kay, "Enterprise Systems Projects: The Role of Liminal Space in Enterprise Systems Implementation," *Journal of Information Technology* 27, no. 4 (December 2012): 259–69, doi:http://dx.doi.org/10.1057/jit.2012.22.

30. van Gennep, *The Rites of Passage*.

31. Turner, *The Ritual Process*.

32. Tony Salvador, Genevieve Bell, and Ken Anderson, "Design Ethnography," *Design Management Journal* (Former Series) 10, no. 4 (October 1999): 41, doi:10.1111/j.1948-7169.1999.tb00274.x.

2. WHAT IS SERVICE DESIGN

1. B. Joseph Pine and James H. Gilmore, *The Experience Economy*, updated ed. (Boston: Harvard Business Review Press, 2011).

2. Adam Smith, *The Wealth of Nations*, ed. Edwin Cannan (New York: Modern Library, 2000), 360.

3. One would hope that Mr. Smith left librarians off his list due to his appreciation for the efforts of these types of "menial laborers" and didn't group them in with buffoons. But intent has been lost to history.

4. Smith, *The Wealth of Nations*, 361.

5. World Bank, "Services, Etc., Value Added (Percentage of GDP)," 2016, http://data.worldbank.org/indicator/NV.SRV.TETC.ZS.

6. Smith, *The Wealth of Nations*, 361.

7. Joe Marquez and Annie Downey, "Service Design: An Introduction to a Holistic Assessment Methodology of Library Services," *Weave: Journal of Library User Experience* 1, no. 2

(2015), doi:http://dx.doi.org/10.3998/weave.12535642.0001.201; G. Lynn Shostack, "How to Design a Service," *European Journal of Marketing* 16, no. 1 (1982): 49–63; G. Lynn Shostack, "Designing Services That Deliver," *Harvard Business Review* 62, no. 1 (February 1984): 133–39; Pine and Gilmore, *The Experience Economy*; Donald A. Norman, "The Way I See It: Systems Thinking: A Product Is More Than the Product," *Interactions* 16, no. 5 (September 2009): 52–54, doi:10.1145/1572626.1572637.

8. Shostack, "How to Design a Service," 49.

9. Andrew Polaine, Lavrans Løvlie, and Ben Reason, eds., *Service Design: From Insight to Implementation* (Brooklyn, N.Y.: Rosenfeld Media, 2013).

10. Computers can fall into either category, although rarely do we ask a computer a question.

11. Mary Jo Bitner, "Servicescapes: The Impact of Physical Surroundings on Customers and Employees," *Journal of Marketing* 56, no. 2 (April 1992): 57–71.

12. U.S. Electoral College, "Electoral Votes for President and Vice President: 1904 Election for the Thirtieth Term," 2016, http://www.archives.gov/federal-register/electoral-college/votes/1905_1909.html#1904.

13. Bitner, "Servicescapes."

14. Pine and Gilmore, *The Experience Economy*, 17.

15. Polaine, Løvlie, and Reason, *Service Design*.

16. Polaine, Løvlie, and Reason, *Service Design*, 134.

17. Polaine, Løvlie, and Reason, *Service Design*.

18. Pine and Gilmore, *The Experience Economy*.

19. Yi-Fu Tuan, *Space and Place: The Perspective of Experience* (Minneapolis: University of Minnesota Press, 1989), 8.

20. Polaine, Løvlie, and Reason, *Service Design*.

21. Polaine, Løvlie, and Reason, *Service Design*, 36.

22. Tom Guarriello, "Experiencing Experience," *UX Magazine*, October 10, 2006, https://uxmag.com/articles/101/experiencing-and-designing-experience.

23. Genevieve Bell and Joseph Kaye, "Designing Technology for Domestic Spaces: A Kitchen Manifesto," *Gastronomica: The Journal of Food and Culture* 2, no. 2 (May 2002): 46–62, doi:10.1525/gfc.2002.2.2.46.

24. Andrew Hinton, *Understanding Context: Environment, Language, and Information Architecture* (Beijing: O'Reilly, 2015).

25. Pine and Gilmore, *The Experience Economy*.

26. Pine and Gilmore, *The Experience Economy*.

27. John Maeda, *The Laws of Simplicity* (Cambridge, Mass.: MIT Press, 2006); Donald A. Norman, "Designing Waits That Work," *MIT Sloan Management Review*, Summer 2009, http://sloanreview.mit.edu/article/designing-waits-that-work/.

28. Maeda, *The Laws of Simplicity* 58.

29. Bitner, "Servicescapes."

30. Charles Willard Moore and Kevin P. Keim, eds., *You Have to Pay for the Public Life: Selected Essays of Charles W. Moore* (Cambridge, Mass.: MIT Press, 2004), 95.

31. Moore and Keim, *You Have to Pay for the Public Life*.

32. Bitner, "Servicescapes."

33. Mary Jo Bitner, "Evaluating Service Encounters: The Effects of Physical Surroundings and Employee Responses," *Journal of Marketing* 54, no. 2 (April 1990): 69–82.

34. Donlyn Lyndon, "Participation," in *You Have to Pay for the Public Life: Selected Essays of Charles W. Moore*, ed. Charles Willard Moore and Kevin P. Keim (Cambridge, Mass.: MIT Press, 2004), 98.

35. Andrew Polaine, "Designing for Services beyond the Screen," *A List Apart*, June 25, 2013, http://alistapart.com/article/designing-for-services-beyond-the-screen.

36. Steve Krug, *Don't Make Me Think, Revisited: A Common Sense Approach to Web Usability*, 3rd ed. (Berkeley, Calif.: New Riders, 2014), 63.

37. A channel is any method used to exchange information with the user. In the case of a library, a user may be confronted with virtual (e.g., website, chat, e-mail) and physical channels (e.g., the physical library with physical touchpoints).

38. Marquez and Downey, "Service Design," para. 5.

39. Stefan Holmlid, "Participative, Co-Operative, Emancipatory: From Participatory Design to Service Design," in *First Nordic Conference on Service Design and Service Innovation, Oslo, Norway* vol. 5 (2009), https://www.researchgate.net/publication/228629923_Participative_co-operative_emancipatory_From_participatory_design_to_service_design.

40. Fred Dust and Gitte Jonsdatter, "Participatory Design," in *Design Dictionary*, ed. Michael Erlhoff and Tim Marshall, Board of International Research in Design (Berlin: Birkhäuser Basel, 2008), 290–93, doi:http://link.springer.com/referenceworkentry/10.1007.978-3-7643-8140-0_193.

41. Birgit Mager, "Service Design," in *Design Dictionary*, ed. Michael Erlhoff and Tim Marshall, Board of International Research in Design (Berlin: Birkhäuser Basel, 2008), 354–57, doi:http://dx.doi.org/10.1007.978-3-7643-8140-0_244.

42. Marquez and Downey, "Service Design," para. 8.

43. Marc Stickdorn and Jakob Schneider, *This Is Service Design Thinking: Basics, Tools, Cases* (Hoboken, N.J.: Wiley, 2011).

44. Marc Steen, Menno Manschot, and De Koning, "Benefits of Co-Design in Service Design Projects," *International Journal of Design* 5, no. 2 (2011): 53–60.

45. Stickdorn and Schneider, *This Is Service Design Thinking*, 40.

46. Marquez and Downey, "Service Design," paragraph 17.

47. John S. Hammond, Ralph L. Keeney, and Howard Raiffa, "The Hidden Traps in Decision Making," *Harvard Business Review* 84, no. 1 (January 2006): 47–58.

48. Pine and Gilmore, *The Experience Economy*.

49. Livework Intelligence, "How People Cluster Experiences in Their Life," *Livework*, October 21, 2015, http://liveworkstudio.com/intelligence/how-people-cluster-experiences-in-their-life/.

50. Stickdorn and Schneider, *This Is Service Design Thinking*.

51. Pine and Gilmore, *The Experience Economy*, 154.

52. Alexander von Humboldt and Aimé Bonpland, *Essay on the Geography of Plants*, ed. Stephen T. Jackson, trans. Sylvie Romanowski (Chicago: University of Chicago Press, 2008), 79.

53. Jon Kolko, *Well-Designed: How to Use Empathy to Create Products People Love* (Boston: Harvard Business Review Press, 2014), 75.

54. Tim Brown, "Design Thinking," *Harvard Business Review* 86, no. 6 (June 2008): 87.

55. Kolko, *Well-Designed*.

56. Dev Patnaik, *Wired to Care: How Companies Prosper When They Create Widespread Empathy* (Upper Saddle River, N.J.: FT Press, 2009), 8.

57. Cindy Tripp, "No Empathy, No Service," *Design Management Review* 24, no. 3 (2013): 64.

58. Polaine, "Designing for Services beyond the Screen," paragraph 7.

59. Tom Kelley, *The Ten Faces of Innovation: IDEO's Strategies for Beating the Devil's Advocate and Driving Creativity throughout Your Organization* (New York: Currency/Doubleday, 2005).

60. Bonnie Prince Billy, "Where Is the Puzzle?" *Lie Down in the Light*, 2008, Domino Recording, *Song Lyrics*, http://www.songlyrics.com/bonnie-prince-billy/where-is-the-puzzle-lyrics/.

61. Christian Madsbjerg and Mikkel B. Rasmussen, *The Moment of Clarity: Using the Human Sciences to Solve Your Hardest Business Problems* (Boston: Harvard Business Review Press, 2014).

62. Polaine, Løvlie, and Reason, *Service Design*, 132.

3. SERVICE DESIGN, IN PRACTICE

1. Lewis Carroll, Roger Lancelyn Green, and John Tenniel, *Alice's Adventures in Wonderland: And, Through the Looking-Glass and What Alice Found There* (New York: Oxford University Press, 1998), 106.

2. Fabian Segelström, "Visualizations in Service Design," Ph.D. dissertation, Linköping Institute of Technology, Linköping University, 2010, 1, https://www.diva-portal.org/smash/get/diva2:354845/FULLTEXT01.pdf.

3. Susan Meyer Goldstein, et al., "The Service Concept: The Missing Link in Service Design Research?" *Journal of Operations Management* 20, no. 2 (April 2002): 121–34, doi:10.1016/S0272-6963(01)00090-0.

4. Larry Leifer, "Design-Team Performance: Metrics and the Impact of Technology," in *Evaluating Corporate Training: Models and Issues*, ed. Stephen M. Brown and Constance J. Seidner (Boston: Kluwer Academic, 1998), 297–319, http://link.springer.com/chapter/10.1007%2F978-94-011-4850-4_14#page-1.

5. Tom Kelley, *The Ten Faces of Innovation: IDEO's Strategies for Beating the Devil's Advocate and Driving Creativity throughout Your Organization* (New York: Currency/Doubleday, 2005), 137.

6. Kelley, *The Ten Faces of Innovation*, 16–17.

7. Andrew Polaine, Lavrans Løvlie, and Ben Reason, eds., *Service Design: From Insight to Implementation* (Brooklyn, N.Y.: Rosenfeld Media, 2013).

8. Joe Marquez, Annie Downey, and Ryan Clement, "Walking a Mile in the User's Shoes: Customer Journey Mapping as a Method to Understanding the User Experience," *Internet Reference Services Quarterly* 20, no. 3/4 (2015): 135–50, doi:10.1080/10875301.2015.1107000.

9. Joe Marquez and Annie Downey, "Service Design: An Introduction to a Holistic Assessment Methodology of Library Services," *Weave: Journal of Library User Experience* 1, no. 2 (2015): para. 23, doi:http://dx.doi.org/10.3998/weave.12535642.0001.201.

4. TOOLS AND TECHNIQUES

1. Andrew Polaine, Lavrans Løvlie, and Ben Reason, eds., *Service Design: From Insight to Implementation* (Brooklyn, N.Y.: Rosenfeld Media, 2013).

2. Donald A. Norman, *Turn Signals Are the Facial Expressions of Automobiles* (Reading, Mass.: Addison-Wesley, 1992), 19.

3. Polaine, Løvlie, and Reason, *Service Design*.

4. Polaine, Løvlie, and Reason, *Service Design*.

5. Courtney Greene McDonald, *Putting the User First: 30 Strategies for Transforming Library Services* (Chicago: Association of College and Research Libraries, a division of the American Library Association, 2014).

6. "Suma," *North Carolina State University Libraries*, https://www.lib.ncsu.edu/reports/suma.

7. Steve Portigal, *Interviewing Users: How to Uncover Compelling Insights* (Brooklyn, N.Y.: Rosenfeld Media, 2013).

8. Polaine, Løvlie, and Reason, *Service Design*.

9. Portigal, *Interviewing Users*.

10. Kim Goodwin and Alan Cooper, *Designing for the Digital Age: How to Create Human-Centered Products and Services* (Indianapolis, Ind.: Wiley, 2009).

11. Edgar H. Schein, *The Corporate Culture Survival Guide: Sense and Nonsense about Culture Change* (San Francisco, Calif.: Jossey-Bass, 1999), 86.

12. Pazit Ben-Nun, "Respondent Fatigue," in *Encyclopedia of Survey Research Methods*, ed. Paul J. Lavrakas (Thousand Oaks, Calif.: Sage, 2008), 743–44.

13. Stephen R. Porter, Michael E. Whitcomb, and William H. Weitzer, "Multiple Surveys of Students and Survey Fatigue," *New Directions for Institutional Research* 121 (January 2004): 63–73, doi:10.1002/ir.101.

14. Goodwin and Cooper, *Designing for the Digital Age.*

15. Goodwin and Cooper, *Designing for the Digital Age,* 231.

16. Goodwin and Cooper, *Designing for the Digital Age,* 238.

17. Solomon E. Asch, "Opinions and Social Pressure," *Readings about the Social Animal* 193 (1955): 17–26.

18. Tony Salvador, Genevieve Bell, and Ken Anderson, "Design Ethnography," *Design Management Journal* (Former Series) 10, no. 4 (October 1999): 41, doi:10.1111/j.1948-7169.1999.tb00274.x.

19. Brigitte Jordan, "Transforming Ethnography, Reinventing Research," *Field Methods* 9, no. 3 (August 1997): 12, doi:10.1177/1525822X970090030201.

20. Andrew Crabtree, Mark Rouncefield, and Peter Tolmie, "Design Ethnography in a Nutshell," in *Doing Design Ethnography,* Human–Computer Interaction Series (London: Springer, 2012), 183–205.

21. Crabtree, Rouncefield, and Tolmie, "Design Ethnography in a Nutshell," 189.

22. Crabtree, Rouncefield, and Tolmie, "Design Ethnography in a Nutshell," 190.

23. Clifford Geertz, *The Interpretation of Cultures: Selected Essays* (New York: Basic Books, 1973), 5.

24. Christian Madsbjerg and Mikkel B. Rasmussen, "An Anthropologist Walks into a Bar . . ." *Harvard Business Review* 92, no. 3 (March 2014): 80–88.

25. Salvador, Bell, and Anderson, "Design Ethnography."

26. Crabtree, Rouncefield, and Tolmie, "Design Ethnography in a Nutshell."

27. Joe Marquez, Annie Downey, and Ryan Clement, "Walking a Mile in the User's Shoes: Customer Journey Mapping as a Method to Understanding the User Experience," *Internet Reference Services Quarterly* 20, no. 3/4 (2015): 135–50, doi:10.1080/10875301.2015.1107000.

28. Chris Risdon, "The Journey from Products to Services," in *Service Design: From Insight to Implementation,* ed. Andrew Polaine, Lavrans Løvlie, and Ben Reason (Brooklyn, N.Y.: Rosenfeld Media, 2013), 103–5.

29. Risdon, "The Journey from Products to Services," 104.

30. Risdon, "The Journey from Products to Services," 104.

31. Marquez, Downey, and Clement, "Walking a Mile in the User's Shoes."

32. Joe Marquez and Annie Downey, "Service Design: An Introduction to a Holistic Assessment Methodology of Library Services," *Weave: Journal of Library User Experience* 1, no. 2 (2015): para. 25, doi:http://dx.doi.org/10.3998/weave.12535642.0001.201.

33. Don H. Zimmerman and D. Lawrence Wieder, "The Diary: 'Diary-Interview Method,'" *Urban Life* 5, no. 4 (January 1977): 485.

34. Zimmerman and Wieder, "The Diary."

35. Zimmerman and Wieder, "The Diary," 481.

36. Katie Clark, "Mapping Diaries, or Where Do They Go All Day?" *Studying Students: The Undergraduate Research Project at the University of Rochester,* ed. Nancy Fried Foster and Susan Gibbons (Chicago: Association of College and Research Libraries, 2010), 48–54,https://urresearch.rochester.edu/institutionalPublicationPublicView.action?institutionalItemId=7044.

37. D. R. Gross, "Time Allocation: A Tool for the Study of Cultural Behavior," *Annual Review of Anthropology* 13, no. 1 (1984): 519, doi:10.1146/annurev.an.13.100184.002511.

38. We approached our administrative assistant, and she informed us that Facilities was scheduled to clean out the outlets as part of their annual maintenance of the library. The chairs, however, were a different issue. We discovered that as chairs break, they are reassembled using parts from previously broken chairs. This reassembling of chairs results in Franken-chairs. While they may look the same, the chairs are actually different heights depending on how the legs were cut. The end result is that some chairs will get stuck under tables if pushed in too far. And Reserves and ILL were already in the process, at the time the diary was written, of updating scanning procedures. This was informative because the research team learned bits and

pieces about the library as a result of our inquiries. We might not have learned about the outlets, the chairs, or even the updating of scanning procedures had we not inquired.

39. Marc Stickdorn and Jakob Schneider, *This Is Service Design Thinking: Basics, Tools, Cases* (Hoboken, N.J.: Wiley, 2011), 166.

40. Taiichi Ohno, "Ask 'Why' Five Times about Every Matter," *Toyota Global*, March 2006, para. 1, http://www.toyota-global.com/company/toyota_traditions/quality/mar_apr_ 2006.html.

41. Tom Kelley, *The Ten Faces of Innovation: IDEO's Strategies for Beating the Devil's Advocate and Driving Creativity throughout Your Organization* (New York: Currency/Doubleday, 2005), 46.

42. Polaine, Løvlie, and Reason, *Service Design*, 140.

43. Tim Brown, "Design Thinking," *Harvard Business Review* 86, no. 6 (June 2008): 87.

44. Polaine, Løvlie, and Reason, *Service Design*.

45. Bella Martin and Bruce M. Hanington, *Universal Methods of Design: 100 Ways to Research Complex Problems, Develop Innovative Ideas, and Design Effective Solutions*, digital ed. (Beverly, Mass.: Rockport Publishers, 2012), 96.

46. Portigal, *Interviewing Users*.

47. Jon Kolko, *Well-Designed: How to Use Empathy to Create Products People Love* (Boston: Harvard Business Review Press, 2014).

48. Kolko, *Well-Designed*.

49. Rebecca Blakiston, *Usability Testing: A Practical Guide for Librarians*, Practical Guides for Librarians, No. 11 (Lanham, Md.: Rowman & Littlefield, 2015).

50. In his book *Well-Designed*, John Kolko suggests a combination of moving utterances into a spreadsheet and then, through a mail-merge process, moving those cells (containing single utterances) to a word processing document. These can then be cut and pasted to the synthesis wall. This sounds like a great method. We encourage you to explore what method works best for you and your team.

51. Janet Smithson, "Focus Groups," in *The Sage Handbook of Social Research Methods*, ed. Pertti Alasuutari, Leonard Bickman, and Julia Brannen (London: Sage, 2008), 357–70.

52. Smithson, "Focus Groups."

53. Smithson, "Focus Groups."

54. Asch, "Opinions and Social Pressure"; Janet Smithson, "Using and Analysing Focus Groups: Limitations and Possibilities," *International Journal of Social Research Methodology* 3, no. 2 (2000): 103–19.

55. G. Lynn Shostack, "Designing Services That Deliver," *Harvard Business Review* 62, no. 1 (February 1984): 135.

56. Marquez and Downey, "Service Design."

57. Marquez and Downey, "Service Design."

58. Shostack, "Designing Services That Deliver," 135.

59. Polaine, Løvlie, and Reason, *Service Design*.

5. ADAPTING SERVICE DESIGN
TO YOUR LIBRARY

1. Joe Marquez and Annie Downey, "Service Design: Toward a Holistic Assessment of the Library," *PNLA Quarterly* 80, no. 1 (2015): 37–47, http://www.pnla.org/assets/Quarterly/ marquezdowney_pnla2015.pdf.

2. Charles Willard Moore and Kevin P. Keim, eds., *You Have to Pay for the Public Life: Selected Essays of Charles W. Moore* (Cambridge, Mass.: MIT Press, 2004).

3. Malcolm McCullough, *Digital Ground: Architecture, Pervasive Computing, and Environmental Knowing* (Cambridge, Mass.: MIT Press, 2005).

4. Edgar H. Schein, *The Corporate Culture Survival Guide: Sense and Nonsense about Culture Change* (San Francisco, Calif.: Jossey-Bass, 1999).

5. While the authors have no firsthand knowledge of what it was like to witness a bronto-saurus move, they do agree that such a large and cumbersome creature might not have been one of the most nimble of dinosaurs.

6. Schein, *The Corporate Culture Survival Guide.*

7. Carol Duncan, *Civilizing Rituals: Inside Public Art Museums*, Re Visions: Critical Studies in the History and Theory of Art Series (London and New York: Routledge, 1995), 1–2.

8. Jane Jacobs, *The Death and Life of Great American Cities* (New York: Vintage Books, 1992), 15.

6. LOOKING FORWARD

1. "Do. Or do not. There is no try."—Yoda from *The Empire Strikes Back.*

Bibliography

Asch, Solomon E. "Opinions and Social Pressure." *Readings about the Social Animal* 193 (1955): 17–26.

Bell, Genevieve. "Making Sense of Museums: The Museum as Cultural Ecology.'" *Intel Labs* 1 (2002): 1–17.

Bell, Genevieve, and Joseph Kaye. "Designing Technology for Domestic Spaces: A Kitchen Manifesto." *Gastronomica: The Journal of Food and Culture* 2, no. 2 (May 2002): 46–62, doi:10.1525/gfc.2002.2.2.46.

Ben-Nun, Pazit. "Respondent Fatigue." In *Encyclopedia of Survey Research Methods*, ed. Paul J. Lavrakas, 743–44. Thousand Oaks, Calif.: Sage, 2008.

Billy, Bonnie Prince. "Where Is the Puzzle?" *Lie Down in the Light*, 2008, Domino Recording, *Song Lyrics*, http://www.songlyrics.com/bonnie-prince-billy/where-is-the-puzzle-lyrics/.

Bitner, Mary Jo. "Evaluating Service Encounters: The Effects of Physical Surroundings and Employee Responses." *Journal of Marketing* 54, no. 2 (April 1990): 69–82.

———. "Servicescapes: The Impact of Physical Surroundings on Customers and Employees." *Journal of Marketing* 56, no. 2 (April 1992): 57–71.

Blakiston, Rebecca. *Usability Testing: A Practical Guide for Librarians*, Practical Guides for Librarians, No. 11. Lanham, Md.: Rowman & Littlefield, 2015.

Brown, Tim. *Change by Design: How Design Thinking Transforms Organizations and Inspires Innovation*. New York: Harper Business, 2009.

———. "Design Thinking." *Harvard Business Review* 86, no. 6 (June 2008): 84–92.

Carroll, Lewis, Roger Lancelyn Green, and John Tenniel. *Alice's Adventures in Wonderland: And, Through the Looking-Glass and What Alice Found There*. New York: Oxford University Press, 1998.

Christensen, Clayton M., and Michael E. Raynor. *The Innovator's Solution: Creating and Sustaining Successful Growth*. Boston: Harvard Business Review Press, 2013.

Clark, Katie. "Mapping Diaries, or Where Do They Go All Day?" *Studying Students: The Undergraduate Research Project at the University of Rochester*, ed. Nancy Fried Foster and Susan Gibbons, 48–54. Chicago: Association of College and Research Libraries, 2010, https://urresearch.rochester.edu/institutionalPublicationPublicView.action?institutionalItemId=7044.

Crabtree, Andrew, Mark Rouncefield, and Peter Tolmie. "Design Ethnography in a Nutshell." In *Doing Design Ethnography*, Human–Computer Interaction Series, 183–205. London: Springer, 2012.

Dreyfuss, Henry. "The Industrial Designer and the Businessman." *Harvard Business Review* 28, no. 6 (November 1950): 77–85.

Duncan, Carol. *Civilizing Rituals: Inside Public Art Museums*, Re Visions: Critical Studies in the History and Theory of Art Series. London and New York: Routledge, 1995.

Dust, Fred, and Gitte Jonsdatter. "Participatory Design." In *Design Dictionary*, ed. Michael Erlhoff and Tim Marshall, Board of International Research in Design, 90–93. Berlin: Birkhäuser Basel, 2008, doi:http://link.springer.com/referenceworkentry/10.1007.978-3-7643-8140-0_193.

Geertz, Clifford. "The Bazaar Economy: Information and Search in Peasant Marketing." *American Economic Review* 68, no. 2 (May 1978): 28–32.

———. *The Interpretation of Cultures: Selected Essays*. New York: Basic Books, 1973.

Goldstein, Susan Meyer, et al. "The Service Concept: The Missing Link in Service Design Research?" *Journal of Operations Management* 20, no. 2 (April 2002): 121–34, doi:10.1016/S0272-6963(01)00090-0.

Goodwin, Kim, and Alan Cooper. *Designing for the Digital Age: How to Create Human-Centered Products and Services*. Indianapolis, Ind.: Wiley, 2009.

Gross, D. R. "Time Allocation: A Tool for the Study of Cultural Behavior." *Annual Review of Anthropology* 13, no. 1 (1984): 519–58, doi:10.1146/annurev.an.13.100184.002511.

Guarriello, Tom. "Experiencing Experience." *UX Magazine*, October 10, 2006, https://uxmag.com/articles/101/experiencing-and-designing-experience.

Hammond, John S., Ralph L. Keeney, and Howard Raiffa. "The Hidden Traps in Decision Making." *Harvard Business Review* 84, no. 1 (January 2006): 47–58.

Hinton, Andrew. *Understanding Context: Environment, Language, and Information Architecture*. Beijing: O'Reilly, 2015.

Holmlid, Stefan. "Participative, Co-Operative, Emancipatory: From Participatory Design to Service Design." In *First Nordic Conference on Service Design and Service Innovation, Oslo, Norway* vol. 5 (2009), https://www.researchgate.net/publication/228629923_Participative_co-operative_emancipatory_From_participatory_design_to_service_design.

Jacobs, Jane. *The Death and Life of Great American Cities*. New York: Vintage Books, 1992.

Jordan, Brigitte. "Transforming Ethnography, Reinventing Research." *Field Methods* 9, no. 3 (August 1997): 12–17, doi:10.1177/1525822X970090030201.

Kelley, Tom. *The Ten Faces of Innovation: IDEO's Strategies for Beating the Devil's Advocate and Driving Creativity throughout Your Organization*. New York: Currency/Doubleday, 2005.

Kolko, Jon. *Well-Designed: How to Use Empathy to Create Products People Love*. Boston: Harvard Business Review Press, 2014.

Krug, Steve. *Don't Make Me Think, Revisited: A Common Sense Approach to Web Usability*, 3rd ed. Berkeley, Calif.: New Riders, 2014.

Leifer, Larry. "Design-Team Performance: Metrics and the Impact of Technology." In *Evaluating Corporate Training: Models and Issues*, ed. Stephen M. Brown and Constance J. Seidner, 397–319. Boston: Kluwer Academic, 1998, http://link.springer.com/chapter/10.1007%2F978-94-011-4850-4_14#page-1.

Livework Intelligence. "How People Cluster Experiences in Their Life." *Livework*, October 21, 2015, http://liveworkstudio.com/intelligence/how-people-cluster-experiences-in-their-life/.

Lyndon, Donlyn. "Participation." In *You Have to Pay for the Public Life: Selected Essays of Charles W. Moore*, ed. Charles Willard Moore and Kevin P. Keim, 94–98. Cambridge, Mass.: MIT Press, 2004.

Madsbjerg, Christian, and Mikkel B. Rasmussen. "An Anthropologist Walks into a Bar . . ." *Harvard Business Review* 92, no. 3 (March 2014): 80–88.

———. *The Moment of Clarity: Using the Human Sciences to Solve Your Hardest Business Problems*. Boston: Harvard Business Review Press, 2014.

Maeda, John. *The Laws of Simplicity*. Cambridge, Mass.: MIT Press, 2006.

Mager, Birgit. "Service Design." In *Design Dictionary*, ed. Michael Erlhoff and Tim Marshall, Board of International Research in Design, 354–57. Berlin: Birkhäuser Basel, 2008, doi:http://dx.doi.org/10.1007.978-3-7643-8140-0_244.

Marquez, Joe, and Annie Downey. "Service Design: An Introduction to a Holistic Assessment Methodology of Library Services." *Weave: Journal of Library User Experience* 1, no. 2 (2015), doi:http://dx.doi.org/10.3998/weave.12535642.0001.201.

———. "Service Design: Toward a Holistic Assessment of the Library." *PNLA Quarterly* 80, no. 1 (2015): 37–47, http://www.pnla.org/assets/Quarterly/marquezdowney_pnla2015.pdf.

Marquez, Joe, Annie Downey, and Ryan Clement. "Walking a Mile in the User's Shoes: Customer Journey Mapping as a Method to Understanding the User Experience." *Internet Reference Services Quarterly* 20, no. 3/4 (2015): 135–50, doi:10.1080/10875301.2015.1107000.

Martin, Bella, and Bruce M. Hanington. *Universal Methods of Design: 100 Ways to Research Complex Problems, Develop Innovative Ideas, and Design Effective Solutions*, digital ed. Beverly, Mass.: Rockport Publishers, 2012.

McCullough, Malcolm. *Digital Ground: Architecture, Pervasive Computing, and Environmental Knowing*. Cambridge, Mass.: MIT Press, 2005.

McDonald, Courtney Greene. *Putting the User First: 30 Strategies for Transforming Library Services*. Chicago: Association of College and Research Libraries, a division of the American Library Association, 2014.

Meadows, Donella H. *Thinking in Systems: A Primer*. White River Junction, Vt.: Chelsea Green, 2008.

Meyer, Christopher, and Andre Schwager. "Understanding Customer Experience." *Harvard Business Review* 85, no. 2 (February 2007): 117–26.

Moore, Charles Willard, and Kevin P. Keim, eds. *You Have to Pay for the Public Life: Selected Essays of Charles W. Moore*. Cambridge, Mass.: MIT Press, 2004.

Morville, Peter. *Intertwingled: Information Changes Everything*. Ann Arbor, Mich.: Semantic Studios, 2014.

Norman, Donald A. "Designing Waits That Work." *MIT Sloan Management Review*, Summer 2009, http://sloanreview.mit.edu/article/designing-waits-that-work/.

———. *Turn Signals Are the Facial Expressions of Automobiles*. Reading, Mass.: Addison-Wesley, 1992.

———. "The Way I See It: Systems Thinking; A Product Is More Than the Product." *Interactions* 16, no. 5 (September 2009): 52–54, doi:10.1145/1572626.1572637.

Ohno, Taiichi. "Ask 'Why' Five Times about Every Matter." *Toyota Global*, March 2006, para. 1, http://www.toyota-global.com/company/toyota_traditions/quality/mar_apr_2006.html.

Patnaik, Dev. *Wired to Care : How Companies Prosper When They Create Widespread Empathy*. Upper Saddle River, N.J.: FT Press, 2009.

Pine, B. Joseph, and James H. Gilmore. *The Experience Economy*, updated ed. Boston: Harvard Business Review Press, 2011.

Polaine, Andrew. "Designing for Services beyond the Screen." *A List Apart*, June 25, 2013, http://alistapart.com/article/designing-for-services-beyond-the-screen.

Polaine, Andrew, Lavrans Løvlie, and Ben Reason, eds. *Service Design: From Insight to Implementation*. Brooklyn, N.Y.: Rosenfeld Media, 2013.

Porter, Stephen R., Michael E. Whitcomb, and William H. Weitzer. "Multiple Surveys of Students and Survey Fatigue." *New Directions for Institutional Research* 121 (January 2004): 63–73, doi:10.1002/ir.101.

Portigal, Steve. *Interviewing Users: How to Uncover Compelling Insights*. Brooklyn, N.Y.: Rosenfeld Media, 2013.

Risdon, Chris. "The Journey from Products to Services." In *Service Design: From Insight to Implementation*, ed. Andrew Polaine, Lavrans Løvlie, and Ben Reason. Brooklyn, N.Y.: Rosenfeld Media, 2013.

Salvador, Tony, Genevieve Bell, and Ken Anderson. "Design Ethnography." *Design Management Journal* (Former Series) 10, no. 4 (October 1999): 36–41, doi:10.1111/j.1948-7169.1999.tb00274.x.

Schein, Edgar H. *The Corporate Culture Survival Guide: Sense and Nonsense about Culture Change*. San Francisco, Calif.: Jossey-Bass, 1999.

Segelström, Fabian. "Visualizations in Service Design." Ph.D. dissertation, Linköping Institute of Technology, Linköping University, 2010, 1, https://www.diva-portal.org/smash/get/diva2:354845/FULLTEXT01.pdf.

Senge, Peter M. *The Fifth Discipline: The Art and Practice of the Learning Organization*, rev. and updated ed. New York: Doubleday/Currency, 2006.

Shostack, G. Lynn. "Designing Services That Deliver." *Harvard Business Review* 62, no. 1 (February 1984): 133–39.

———. "How to Design a Service." *European Journal of Marketing* 16, no. 1 (1982): 49–63.

Smith, Adam. *The Wealth of Nations*, ed. Edwin Cannan. New York: Modern Library, 2000.

Smithson, Janet. "Focus Groups." In *The Sage Handbook of Social Research Methods*, ed. Pertti Alasuutari, Leonard Bickman, and Julia Brannen, 357–70. London: Sage, 2008.

———. "Using and Analysing Focus Groups: Limitations and Possibilities." *International Journal of Social Research Methodology* 3, no. 2 (2000): 103–19.

Steen, Marc, Menno Manschot, and De Koning. "Benefits of Co-Design in Service Design Projects." *International Journal of Design* 5, no. 2 (2011): 53–60.

Stickdorn, Marc, and Jakob Schneider. *This Is Service Design Thinking: Basics, Tools, Cases.* Hoboken, N.J: Wiley, 2011.

Taylor, Frederick. *The Principles of Scientific Management*. New York: Harper & Brothers, 1911.

Tripp, Cindy. "No Empathy, No Service." *Design Management Review* 24, no. 3 (2013): 58–64

Tuan, Yi-Fu. *Space and Place: The Perspective of Experience*. Minneapolis: University of Minnesota Press, 1989.

Turner, Victor W. *The Ritual Process: Structure and Anti-Structure*. Symbol, Myth, and –Ritual Series. Ithaca, N.Y: Cornell University Press, 1977.

U.S. Electoral College. "Electoral Votes for President and Vice President: 1904 Election for the Thirtieth Term." 2016, http://www.archives.gov/federal-register/electoral-college/votes/1905_1909.html#1904.

van Gennep, Arnold. *The Rites of Passage*. Trans. Monika B. Vizedom and Gabrielle L. Caffee. Chicago: University of Chicago Press, 2001.

von Humboldt, Alexander, and Aimé Bonpland. *Essay on the Geography of Plants*, ed. Stephen T. Jackson, trans. Sylvie Romanowski. Chicago: University of Chicago Press, 2008.

Wagner, Erica L., Sue Newell, and William Kay. "Enterprise Systems Projects: The Role of Liminal Space in Enterprise Systems Implementation." *Journal of Information Technology* 27, no. 4 (December 2012): 259–69, doi:http://dx.doi.org/10.1057/jit.2012.22.

Williams, Daniel R., and Jerry J. Vaske. "The Measurement of Place Attachment: Validity and Generalizability of a Psychometric Approach." *Forest Science* 49, no. 6 (2003): 830–40.

World Bank. "Services, Etc., Value Added (Percentage of GDP)." 2016, http://data.worldbank.org/indicator/NV.SRV.TETC.ZS.

Zimmerman, Don H., and D. Lawrence Wieder. "The Diary: 'Diary-Interview Method.'" *Urban Life* 5, no. 4 (January 1977): 479–98.

Index

access to information, 14, 30. *See also*
   types of services
analysis and synthesis, 91, 92
analysis, 91, 92. *See also* analysis and
   synthesis; synthesis
anatomy of a service, 15. *See also* context;
   inability to be possessed; interaction;
   purpose and function; time
audience, 19, 31

betwixt and between, 9. *See also* liminal
   phase; rite of passage
bibliothecarius habilis, 110
big-picture, 101, 111, 116
blueprint, 26, 50, 50–51, 52, 55, 95–97,
   116; -ing, 11, 25, 47, 50, 95
built environment, 28, 104, 105, 107, 108,
   111
buy-in, 40, 41, 52, 103, 118

CJM (Customer Journey Map), 50, 72–76,
   95–96. *See also* Customer Journey Map
co-create, 25, 46, 48, 50, 53, 64; -ing, 26,
   45, 47, 49
co-production, 18, 26, 31, 77
communication, 6, 28, 36, 37, 38, 41, 42,
   85, 99–100, 117
confirmation, 10–11
confirming with evidence, 27, 29
consistency, 23, 59, 117, 120

context: anatomy of a service, 15, 30; as
   setting, 9, 10, 14, 18, 21, 30, 33, 41, 61,
   62, 64, 70, 86, 99, 104, 110, 111,
   121n3; feedback, 89; in relation to other
   services, 10, 20, 28, 47, 104, 109, 111;
   time, 61. *See also* ecology map; design
   ethnography
contextual inquiry, 60–62, 71; design
   ethnography, 70; interviews, 111
customer journey map (CJM), 11, 25, 26,
   47, 50, 72–76, 95. *See also* CJM

decontextualizing, 91, 92
design ethnography, 25, 45, 70–72. *See*
   also ethnography
devil's advocate, 29
diary, 49, 76, 77, 77–78, 126n38. *See also*
   journaling
discussion group, 37, 43, 44–45, 47, 58,
   60, 68–70, 91
discussion lead, 37, 69, 83
diverse perspectives, 101
documentation, 37, 38, 50, 70
Dreyfuss, Henry, 1
duration, 11, 20, 21, 30, 52. *See also* time

ecology, 2, 8, 9, 19, 25, 27, 28, 43, 56, 72,
   73, 111; See also ecology map;
   inherited ecology
ecology map, 43, 55–57

About the Authors

Joe J. Marquez is the web services librarian at the Reed College Library. He has presented and written on topics related to service design, UX tools, library space assessment, website usability, and marketing of the library. His current research interests involve service design in the library environment and space usage assessment. Marquez has an MLIS from the University of Washington iSchool, an MBA from Portland State University, and a BA in anthropology from the University of Colorado, Boulder.

Annie Downey is the director of Research Services at the Reed College Library. She has written and presented on user studies, information literacy, K–20 library instruction, assessment, and academic library administration. Her current research interests include critical information literacy, service design in libraries, and the student research process. Downey has an MLS and a PhD in higher education from the University of North Texas.